IN LOVE *with* MALTA

My Gem in the Med

A Guide to the hidden treasures of the
Maltese Islands

PADDY CUMMINS

IN LOVE *with* MALTA

Cover design by

JH Illustration

To all who love

the Maltese Islands.

Contents

IN LOVE *with* MALTA

My Gem in the Med

What is it about the Maltese Islands that brings an Irishman back to these little multi-coloured rocks year after year, fills him with joy and enchantment, and sends him home restored, revitalised, and eagerly looking forward to his next visit? A good question, I hear you say, and one that I suspect thousands of others have asked themselves but can't explain the magnetism of the islands or why they like me, became addicted to this idyllic little spot on the planet.

I first discovered Malta twelve years ago when I was searching around for somewhere to escape to, from the depressing Irish winters when wind, rain, frost and snow were getting me down, dimming my mind and putting extra years on my body. I had enough and was blessed to find this little heaven which I knew was exactly the place I was looking for, my home from home.

I remember my first visit. Approaching from the air, these little sun-drenched dots nestled in the Mediterranean's heart appeared arid and austere, not all that impressive, but when I landed I found a unique and beautiful landscape, a fascinating history and culture, an agreeable climate, and the most friendly, good-natured people in the world.

Maltese landscape is a feast to the eye. Honey coloured rocks, dry stone walls enclosing little farms of greenery, blue ship-laden harbours, yacht-filled marinas, cute little inlets with multi-coloured fishing boats, delightful baroque architecture, magnificent church domes, all bordered by a warm purple blue Mediterranean. It has become my colour postcard, but now I'm happy to share it with a millions of other visitors who come each year, lucky like me to have discovered this little haven.

Being a scribbler and Irish, I suppose it was inevitable that I wouldn't be able to resist the temptation to share the delights of Malta with my readers around the world and in 2013 'It's a Long Way to Malta' (An Irishman's Gem in the Med) was born. I'm thrilled to report that it has become a best-seller on Kindle as an E-Book and on Amazon in paperback and has been helpful for new visitors guiding them to the attractions and charms of the Maltese Islands.

I didn't intend it to be a serious guide book, just a little travel book written in a light vein. I just wanted to share my affection for Malta, an Irishman's take on the places I visited, the characters I met and the fun I enjoyed since I first arrived, but reading the fifty reviews it received; it appears to have given a much appreciated insight to the history and culture of the islands and the charm and personality of the people.

So, still a scribbler and Irish, I have once again succumbed to the temptation of putting pen to paper to share more good news of my little 'Gem in the Med.' This *is* more of a guide book and one that I hope will bring my readers to the heart and soul of Malta. I want to show them the numerous little unspoiled locations that are not widely known, are full of history and intrigue, and will give much pleasure and delight with their beauty and charm.

It is well known that Malta is renowned for its heroic history, exquisite landscape and its charming inhabitants, qualities that feature large in 'It's a Long Way to Malta,' and although not ignoring those wonderful riches in this book, I want to show the hidden pearls of those idyllic islands, a treasure throve of enchantment and pleasure.

I have been amazed to find the Maltese Islands so brimful with hidden gems that are not featured or well known, and I figure that without guidance, it might take visitors several trips to discover them. I have been coming for twelve years and I'm still adding to my collection of 'must visit' beauty spots, little treasures that you won't find in the mainstream guide books, but are well worth seeing, and in my opinion, define the charm and mystique of Malta, Gozo and Comino.

Malta has many fine bustling cities and towns. The capital, the World Heritage City of Valletta, is an amazing example of baroque architecture and is a wonderful testament to the artistry of The Knights who built it all those centuries ago. Today it stands majestically in all its beauty and splendour adorned with magnificent palaces, richly embellished churches and old world shops and restaurants.

Throughout the islands you will also find lots of sleepy villages and picturesque little fishing ports. But Malta can be lively and modern too with a myriad of restaurants, cafes, clubs and nightlife. There is something for everyone to enjoy from living it up in modern urban resorts to meandering at your leisure in little traditional hamlets and villages dotted throughout the islands where time seems to stand still and you can linger awhile and relax in the warm sunshine.

So, come with me on a trek through this ancient paradise of history, beauty and intrigue. If like me, you are addicted to exquisite beauty, fascinated by rich culture or enchanted by warm friendly people, then a stroll through these delightful little islands will fill you with pleasure, gladden your heart and leave you eagerly looking forward to your next visit to the Maltese Islands.

The Maltese Islands

You will find the Maltese Islands of Malta, Gozo and Comino glistening in the centre of the Mediterranean, 90 km south of the Italian island of Sicily and roughly 300 km north of Africa. The three islands have a population of around 450,000 in an area of about 320 square kilometres.

Malta is by far the largest island measuring 21 km by 14 km with 420,000 inhabitants and is the main administrative and commercial centre of the islands. Here I can soak up 7,000 years of intriguing history, enjoy spectacular baroque architecture, and relish all year sunshine across the most exquisite land and seascape. It's a feast to the eye and a joy to the heart. Everywhere I see honey-coloured stone walls, a coastline of cute little coves, startling high cliffs, quiet sandy bays, all lovingly embraced by the deepest blue Mediterranean.

Malta is like a big fascinating outdoor museum. Relics of its astonishing past are clearly visible for me to see and I can delve into millennia of incredible history, explore the amazing feats and legacy of the Knights of St John, or walk in the footsteps of St Paul, the shipwreck survivor who became Malta's patron saint. With all of that exhilarating activity I can never become bored in Malta. Each day I find a new delight, some quaint little spot to explore, a little hamlet or a cosy sheltered beach to rest and be massaged by the soothing sunshine.

Gozo is the second largest island, 14 km by 6 km, with 30,000 souls, greener, quieter, more casual and relaxing and a delight to wander at my leisure. I never tire of visiting Malta's little sister where I feel time stands still, where the people are so genuinely friendly and charming and where the welcome I get is so warm and wonderful. I also get a strong sense of the religious piety of the people of Gozo. Beautiful churches adorn every little village, the Ta Pinu Sanctuary is now a world renowned pilgrimage centre and the Church of St George in Victoria is one of the most richly adorned churches in Europe. The landscape too is a joy to behold. Little farmsteads surrounded by greenery and dry stone walls, villages untouched by time, a craggy coastline of abstract beauty and a network of winding roads that always end at the edge of the blue Mediterranean.

Comino, the smallest island, is virtually uninhabited except in summer when it comes to life with an influx of divers, boaters and nature lovers. Perched midway between Malta and Gozo and measuring only 2.5 square km, it is a delight to visit for its sense of tranquillity, peace and solitude. There isn't much to explore on this tiny barren rock, one hotel, an ancient church and a watchtower built by the Knights several centuries ago.

The Blue Lagoon is Comino's great attraction. This little cove is famous for its unique turquoise waters floating over a bed of white sand and is a life-changing experience for swimmers and snorkelers. Scuba divers find the underwater caves irresistible and large numbers flock there to explore the mystique.

Most people, like me, visit Comino as part of a day trip from Malta. I prefer to go in the spring or autumn shoulder seasons to avoid the intense heat. I simply hop on a ferry in St Paul's Bay and enjoy a lovely day, savouring the pleasure of the Blue Lagoon and rambling around this mysterious sun-baked island.

What is it that attracts so many millions of visitors to those little islands peeping up from the great Mediterranean? I don't have the answer to that intriguing question. I guess it's a combination of things, some rare qualities that define the Maltese and make them special and unique. To me, Malta is a magnate, luring me back every year and rewarding me with peace of mind, energy and wellbeing, and a yearning to return for more of their magic recipe.

History

Malta has a long and turbulent history that dates back to the beginning of civilisation. From the Neolithic period through the reigns of the Phoenicians, the Carthaginians, the Romans and the Byzantines, the Maltese experienced a varied set of influences that left their mark on the islands and the evidence of this colourful past can be seen today in some of the world's oldest temples, tombs and ancient structures.

Throughout the islands the number of archaeological sites is amazing. You'll find Megalithic monuments, Punic tombs, Bronze Age dolmens, Roman Villas and temples that are believed to be the oldest free-standing buildings in the world.

I'm not a historian and my grasp of history can be detailed in simple terms, but like others visiting Malta on a regular basis I am always hugely impressed and fascinated by the array of historic evidence of a seven century journey filled with courage, dignity, chivalry and endurance.

I have no intention of going back 5600 years to when the first Megalithic Temples were erected, but if I had, incredibly, they are still to be seen standing here, and are a wonderful tourist attraction. No, my enduring fascination with Maltese history begins in 1565, because what happened then showed the world what the Maltese were made of, reminding all prospective predators, that anyone taking these primitive, timid people for a 'soft touch' needed to think again, and it was the first real test of their spirit, tenacity and resilience. With their backs to the wall they displayed a reservoir of courage that would continue to manifest itself in many future invasions, unfairly perpetrated, but bravely repelled and defeated.

You might say that the present-day cliché: l*ocation, location,* l*ocation,* could be aptly applied to Malta, and probably it was the source of a lot of their troubles. Being stuck on the crossroads of the Mediterranean – a strategic spot in wartime – placed them on the wish list of many greedy predators, and to hold their ground and their little country, they had to fight, defend, and defeat the bullies, and time after time they did this against all the odds, preserving their dignity, and their little island.

When the Knights of the Order of St. John were welcomed to Malta in 1530, it began 268 years of honourable rule by this Military and Hospitaller Order. They were the makings of Malta, and clear evidence of their inspiration, vision and resourcefulness can be seen today in the beautiful 'World Heritage' City of Valletta, the magnificent palaces, and the myriad of superb churches that adorn every corner of the island.

But in May 1565, the lookout soldier spotted the arrival of the dreaded Turkish armada. 40,000 troops were approaching the island, convinced that they could set up shop with impunity, as Malta had only a meagre 8,000 fighting men. This epic event has gone down in history as 'The Great Siege of Malta' and few other historic episodes rival it for sheer heroism, and brilliant military strategy.

The Turks, led by Sultan Suleiman the Magnificent were in for a shock and a rude awakening. A fierce battle began, and for four blood-spilling months, the islanders stood their ground against massive bombardment in a heroic siege that remains legendary to this day.

The Ottomans first attacked Fort St Elmo because of its strategic position in the Grand Harbour. Wave after wave of assaults pounded the Fort for almost a month but the small garrison of Knights bravely held their ground. The invaders then turned their sights on Fort St Angelo where some of the bloodiest battles of this Holy War took place. Fierce attacks were launched on the Fort and on the fortified Three Cities throughout the long, hot summer of 1565.

At one point in the battle, the Ottoman's floated the headless corpses of captured Knights across the Grand Harbour and this barbaric escalation was reciprocated when Ottoman prisoners were executed and their heads used as 'cannon balls' to fire back. Towards the end of the summer, having suffered heavy losses, and with relief forces arriving to bolster Malta's defences, the Ottomans morale began to wane. Trapped, they retreated, having lost thousands of men. The Great Siege ended on 8th September, the feast of the birth of 'Our Lady', and the Maltese have always believed that their deliverance was mainly due to her divine help.

The eighteenth century wasn't all sunshine for Malta either. With the French Revolution, the Knights lost most of their European influence, territory, and financial support, and as more elderly Knights came to retire in Malta, their financial situation became critical. In 1798, Napolean Bonaparte cast his greedy eyes on the little struggling island – a vital link between France and the Middle East for his planned Egyptian campaign. He used a mean little trick to try and hoodwink the Knights, and gain access to the island when, with his large fleet anchored off the coast, he asked for permission to enter the Grand Harbour to replenish the ships with water and other needs. He was only allowed to bring in four ships and having taken that as an insult and a refusal, he forced his way in, took control, and settled down for what he thought would be a long and fruitful stay.

Once again the Maltese mettle was tested, and they found themselves in yet another dog fight. With the help of the British, they managed to evict the French after two years of a fierce and bitter struggle. This put Britain in the driving seat, and in 1800, with the Knights weakened beyond recovery, they took over the administration of the island, staying until 21st September 1964, when they left and gave Malta back her independence. That date is proudly commemorated every year since, as is 13th December 1974, when Malta was declared a Republic.

Of course, no look back at Malta's history, however brief, would be complete without a mention of the two World Wars of the early twentieth century. In the first, (1914-1918) the Maltese were not directly involved in the terrible battles that killed millions. But they were still an important factor, providing aid and sustenance to the allied troops in need of medication and recuperation, after the various battles of the Eastern Mediterranean. They were nicknamed 'the Nurse of the Mediterranean' for the hospital services they provided.

The Second World War was to be totally different, and a much more tragic event for Malta, because only one day after war was declared on Britain and its allies, the island was attacked by Italy, under the Fascist dictator, Mussolini. Once again, the courage of the people was shown in spades, enduring daily bombardments from the air, repelling invasion attempts, and resisting the might of their attackers with nothing but flimsy land, sea, and air defences, and a spirit and determination to endure.

I was amazed to learn that Hitler's desire to invade and set up a base in Malta led him to drop more bombs on the island than on the City of London, and still those brave people resisted wave after wave of aggression from this evil monster. The women and children lived in underground shelters, while the men shouldered the burden of war, with little or no food for anyone, as convoy after convoy, bringing vital supplies from Britain were blown up on the way.

Miraculously, the island was saved and their second 'Great Siege' ended in 1943 when the Italian navy surrendered in the harbours of Malta. Amazingly, the date was 8th September, the same date as the ending of the 'Great Siege' of 1565, another certain sign for the Maltese of the Divine intervention of 'Our Lady', on the occasion of her birthday. In recognition of their courage and bravery during the war, Malta was awarded the George Cross by King George V1, a rare and unique distinction, cherished so much by the Maltese, that it is now proudly etched on their national flag.

For the past fifty years, Malta has developed and prospered. It is now an Independent Democratic Republic, a respected member of the United Nations, the Commonwealth, and the European Union. In recent years many important world figures have visited Malta. In 1989, American President, George Bush and Soviet Union leader, Mikhail Gorbachef met on the island, and in their talks, agreed to end the 'Cold War.' Pope John Paul and Pope Benedict have been here, and in 2005 the 'Commonwealth Conference' brought many dignitaries, including Britain's Queen Elizabeth.

So there you have it. My own little glimpse of Malta's past, a turbulent history, I'm sure you'll agree, that tested its people for their courage, dignity, spirit, perseverance, endurance and character, and in all categories, they were not founding wanting – they passed with flying colours.

The history timeline of the Maltese Islands

5200 BC

Arrival of man on Malta

3200 BC

Building of Megalithic Temples

2000 BC

Invasion of Bronze Age peoples

800 BC

Phoenician colonisation

900 BC

The start of the Iron Age

480 BC

Carthaginian domination

218 BC

Roman domination

60

St Paul shipwrecked on Malta

395

Byzantine occupation

870

Arabs occupy Malta

1090

Norman occupation

1530

Knights of St John arrive in Malta

1561

Inquisition established

1565

The Great Siege of Malta

1566

The founding of Valletta

1798

Napoleon Bonaparte takes Malta from the Knights

1799

Britain takes Malta

1800

The French surrender

1814

Malta becomes a British Crown Colony

1914-1918

First World War

1939-1945

Second World War

1964

Independence within the British Commonwealth

1974

Malta becomes a Republic

1979

British leave Malta

2004

Malta join European Union

2008

Malta joins Euro Zone

Culture

PEOPLE

The culture of Malta has evolved over 7,000 years of amazing history and is a mixture of customs and traditions that are unique to the Maltese people. From prehistoric times the Islanders, isolated and defenceless in the middle of the Mediterranean had to struggle to keep aggressors at bay, sometimes winning brave battles, but often failing to repel the invaders. That's why the island's history is peppered with long periods of foreign domination, before finally gaining its independence and proudly taking its place among the nations of the world.

Those centuries of foreign rule must surely have influenced Maltese culture but it never lowered the dignity, integrity or spirituality of the Maltese people and they remain today renowned worldwide for their friendly nature and generosity.

I'm amazed at how the Maltese, having endured so much, can still preserve their own unique identity. I'm always appreciative of their friendly welcome, their positive outlook on life and their strict adherence to the highest standards at home or at work. They make the most pleasant and welcoming hosts, whether in hotels, shops or in the services, and I would venture to suggest that nowhere else would I be greeted with such warmth, goodwill and genuine sincerity.

RELIGION

Roman Catholicism is the religion of Malta. 98% of the population are Catholics, which makes them one of the most Catholic countries in the world, but although this is recognised in the constitution, the country acknowledges freedom of religion. Many other religious denominations are represented with small but vibrant communities.

I'm always impressed by the devout faith of the Maltese. Their dedication and piety are apparent to all visitors and they take an active part in all church ceremonies. Religion is very important to the Maltese and it is often a central theme of discussion especially on matters such as marriage, divorce, abortion and morality. Children are taught religion in school, and First Communion and Confirmation are memorable days in the life of a family.

It is estimated that there are 365 churches on the Maltese Islands, one for every day of the year. Each town and village has its own beautiful church which is their landmark and their pride and joy.

The Catholic Church in Malta has kept up with modern technology too. In 2012, the Malta Mass App was introduced. This enlightened innovation gives users access to information regarding the schedule of daily and weekend Masses throughout the islands. It enables them to find Mass in the nearest church, indicating the time, location and the language in which the Mass will be celebrated. It also includes the opening time and locality of adoration chapels, daily Scripture readings and reflections on the Gospel.

The App includes time schedules of more than 4,600 Masses held during the week in 365 churches in 70 parishes in Malta and 14 parishes in Gozo. It also provides information on 57 adoration chapels around Malta. The App, which is available from the App Store has been downloaded to tens of thousands of mobile phones, all of which proves that the Maltese take their religion very seriously and it is the most cherished part of their culture.

ST PAUL

It was St Paul who started it all in 60 AD when after being shipwrecked off the coast, he took shelter on the island and in return for the hospitality received, he gave Christianity to the Islanders and they have cherished it ever since.

St Paul is everywhere in Malta. The faithful revere him and throughout the islands his name is proudly linked to most churches and important buildings. Paul's story is amazing and inspiring. From his early life as an Anti-Christ, killing and persecuting followers of Jesus, to one of the greatest evangelists of all time, he has come a long way. Having spent a lifetime teaching, preaching and suffering, he was eventually executed in Rome on June 29th 0067.

It was on that fateful journey to Rome to plead his case before Ceasar that Paul and 276 other seafarers became shipwrecked, and having waded ashore they discovered that their oases was the little island of Malta. The Maltese people welcomed the beleaguered travellers, fed and nourished them for three months until another ship was available, and in return for their kindness Paul cured their sick, gave them the Christian Faith and pledged to guide and protect them for all time. That was a good bargain and ever since both Paul and the Maltese have faithfully adhered to the terms.

The little church that has marked the spot where he first set foot on the island still stands like a beacon in the square of Saint Paul's Bay, reminding all-comers of that momentous moment of history, the miracle rescue of an execution-bound, future renowned saint, and the miraculous conversion of an island people.

This ancient truth was so important that it was worthy of a chapter in no less a volume than the Holy Bible, and the Maltese are not shy in making the world aware of this unique distinction. The Bible reference is displayed in many languages on the perimeter walls of 'Saint Paul's Shipwreck Church.'

When in Malta I like attending Mass in that little church – so small that at the *'sign of peace'* all of the congregation can clasp hands without moving out of their seats. It is certainly unique and I have to say that I always experience a strange spirituality there, uplifting my soul with an injection of something, a mysterious stimulant that stays with me long after I've gone home to Ireland. Saint Paul is now my hero too.

THE VILLAGE FESTA

One of the best examples of Maltese tradition and culture is the village 'Festa', an annual joyous celebration involving the entire community and continuing for several days. The 'Festa' is largely a religious festival, and is held in every village between the months of May and September. Each village has a patron saint and this is the focus of the village feast. On a certain weekend of the year the villagers will decorate the streets with banners and statues dedicated to the saint and for almost a week locals and tourists rejoice and celebrate the feast, culminating in the ceremonial parading of the saint's statue in a joyful procession to every corner of the village.

During the 'Festa' the whole village is decorated and comes alive with numerous events such as fireworks, church services and performances by the local brass band. The streets are full of stall holders selling a variety of food and beverages. Traditional and fast food stands compete with each other, but the big sellers are the much loved Maltese nougat and other local sweet delicacies.

Although the parading of the statue is the ceremonial highlight of each 'Festa', equally exciting is the compulsory fireworks display. Fireworks are a big part of Maltese tradition and nowhere is this better showcased than at the village feast. The show involves noisy displays of sound and colour that light up the night sky.

The village 'Festa' is regarded as the main annual social event of each parish in Malta. It is a celebration of all they hold dear; religion, spirituality, family, friends, food, drink, wellbeing. These special events are not only cherished by the Maltese, but have become great tourist attractions and I am always appreciative of my welcome to join in the festivities and be thrilled and enchanted by these unique experiences.

THE MALTESE CROSS

The Maltese Cross is a very cherished symbol of the Maltese people and the cross has become part of Malta's heritage and culture. Introduced to Malta by the Knights of St. John of Jerusalem upon taking possession of the islands in 1530, it has become a much-cherished symbol of Maltese tradition and heritage. Its eight points denote the eight obligations or aspirations of the Knights, namely "to live in truth, have faith, repent one's sins, have humility, show justice, be merciful, be sincere and whole-hearted, and endure persecution.

The Knights of St. John of Jerusalem, now commonly known as the Knights of Malta, can trace their origin to a group of monks attached to a hospice built in the Holy Lands to aid pilgrims. Over time, the monks started offering armed escort to travellers as they passed through perilous Syrian territory. Following the success of the First Crusade, the Hospitallers evolved into a military order. The link between the Maltese Cross and these islands was forged with the Knights' arrival in Malta in 1530. By then, the Cross had become the established symbol of the Order, and as the Knights set about putting their stamp on these islands through their inspired architectural feats and patronage of the arts, so the Maltese Cross provided the signature to this glorious legacy. The Cross found itself on coats-of-arms, palaces, hospitals, the entrances and gates to various forts and towers, on fortifications as well as on coins, cannon, monuments, churches, paintings and frescoes, furniture, silverware and jewellery.

Today, the Maltese Cross is undoubtedly the single most recognizable symbol of the Maltese Islands. It is therefore no coincidence that this emblem forms part of the logo of a number of local institutions, including the Malta Tourism Authority, Malta Enterprise, and the Islands' flag-carrier, Air Malta, not to mention the national football and rugby teams' official strip. Many Maltese houses still incorporate the Cross in their stone-work. A visit to any souvenir or gift shop will also reveal an array of local crafts adorned with the Maltese Cross especially the world renowned Maltese handmade lace. When I first visited Malta many years ago one of my first purchases was a gold Maltese cross and chain and I still cherish it as my intimate link with Malta.

It seems that the Maltese Cross, a symbol which chivalric warriors first wore with pride hundreds of years ago in faraway lands, has found a permanent home on this little archipelago in the middle of the Mediterranean!

POLITICS IN MALTA

Malta is a Democratic Republic with the President being the head of state. The Prime Minister is head of the government and legislative power is vested in the parliament of Malta. Since independence, the party electoral system has been dominated by two parties, the Nationalist Party and the Labour Party. Power has alternated between the two parties and with support divided almost equally; elections in the 13 constituencies are fiercely contested and usually won or lost by very narrow margins.

Every five years as the election approaches, the political temperature rises with big party rallies every Sunday attracting thousands of supporters, speeches by the leaders promising a brighter future, cheering, chanting, singing their election anthems and celebrating an anticipated victory. This frenzied campaigning continues until election day when the voters turn out in big numbers, cast their votes and wait in the hope that they have helped to elect their party to government.

On 1st May 2004 Malta joined the EU and on 1st January 2008, adopted the Euro as the national currency. The first election after joining the EU was won narrowly by the Nationalist Party and in May 2011 a nationwide referendum was held on the introduction of divorce. It was the first time that a motion which had originated from outside of Cabinet was approved and enacted by Parliament. In March 2013, the slim majority enjoyed by the Nationalists was overturned dramatically with the Labour Party returning to Government after fifteen years in Opposition.

The current Head of State is President Marie Louise Coleiro Preca, a Maltese ex-minister and the 9th President of Malta since her appointment by parliamentary agreement on 4th April 2014. The Prime Minister is Joseph Muscat, the leader of the Labour Party who became head of government when his party won the 2013 general election. The Leader of the Opposition and head of the Nationalist Party is Simon Busuttil, who has led the party since 2013.

LANGUAGE

Malta has two official languages, Maltese and English. Maltese is a language of Semitic origin written in the Latin script and includes many words from English, French and Italian. Italian is a third language that is spoken fluently by many Maltese.

When I listen to the Maltese people speaking in the rich tones of Malti – their own language – I'm always hugely impressed to realise that a people who have been infiltrated by so many other powers over the centuries has managed to retain a unique language and preserve it as a distinct and proud element of their culture.

The Arabs, who inhabited the islands from the 9th to the 13th centuries, had a definite influence on the Maltese language and today that Arabic influence is evident in the language, especially in place names throughout the islands.

In some well-heeled modern countries that I've visited I have experienced some embarrassing language problems. Not so in Malta. For English speaking visitors like me, language is never a problem here. The Maltese people speak my language fluently and are happy to do so, something which I always greatly appreciate, and for me it is one of the great pleasures of holidaying in Malta.

ARTS AND CRAFTS

Malta has long been well known internationally for its arts and crafts tradition, which, having undergone a revival in recent years is today a flourishing and vibrant industry. Crafts, such as lace, knitwear, basket making, glassmaking and filigree have a high cultural value to the islands. Other craft forms, such as weaving and pottery date back to prehistoric times.

Lace making is one of Malta's most revered traditions. Originally associated with wealth and nobility, it is today considered a highly treasured art and a valued commodity. This local tradition is alive and well in Malta and Gozo. A stroll through the streets of any small Gozitan town will likely bring with it the sight of local women on their doorsteps engrossed in this beautiful tradition. Dating back to the time of the Knights of St John, ornamental lace was introduced as a fashion accessory to embellish the clothing of nobles and the aristocracy. The Maltese quickly became deft at this craft and produced fine examples of lace, used by high society and the clergy. As with other local crafts, the motif of the Maltese Cross was added to the lace to make it uniquely Maltese.

Following a decline and subsequent revival of the art during the British period, lace-making became sought after again, boosting its popularity and demand. Today, Maltese lace is a highly valued commodity and rarer examples of the craft fetch excellent prices at auction.

The process of lace-making is a fascinating one to watch. To see this ancient art being practiced in Malta, you can visit the lace-makers in the Ta' Qali crafts village where this beautiful tradition is on show, or in the wonderful craft shop at Fontana near Victoria in Gozo..

A craft that really flourished under the Knights was gold and silver work. Malta's most precious production is filigree and jewellery. The art of filigree can be traced back to ancient Egypt and can be found throughout the

Mediterranean and Asia. Filigree is a delicate art of jewellery that involves the use of fine threads of gold or silver, woven together to create ornate motifs. Unlike most other types of jewelry, filigree is valued more for the artisan's skill than the actual material used.

Malta's filigree legacy dates back to the Phoenicians who spread this technique throughout the Mediterranean and beyond. However, local artisans have made it all their own, with the most prominent motif being the eight pointed Maltese Cross. This ubiquitous symbol is found in different variations, with or without gemstones, gold or silver, and on bracelets, earrings, and brooches. While filigree can be purchased at most jewellery shops around Malta and Gozo, the experience of watching the jewellery being made always fascinates me and something that I always enjoy.

Glass making in Malta began in earnest in 1968 when Michael Harris from the UK set up Mdina Glass and began producing free-formed organic glassware in colours inspired by the sea, sand, earth and sky. It was an instant success due to the strong tourist industry of Malta and has been thriving ever since. Each piece is handmade and is truly a beautiful work of art.

Since opening its doors to become Malta's first glass factory, Mdina Glass has endeavoured to establish and maintain a reputation for artistic innovation, quality and consistency in each and every individual piece of glassware produced by its artisans. The collection of handmade products, made by its specialist craftsmen, includes a myriad of items designed to bring light and colour to any home. The most traditional line of products includes vases and bowls, perfume bottles, solid objects, fused glassware (incl. plates, clocks, house names and numbers, frames etc.) and intricate lamp-work, figurines and shapes.

The Ta' Qali Crafts Village, located in a former RAF wartime air-field, a few miles from Mdina and Rabat, is the perfect place to see craftsmen and artisans at work on traditional Maltese crafts. Lace making, filigree and glass blowing can all be seen here in this historic old-world setting and spending a day there in the presence of those wonderful artists is a joy to behold, and always a highlight of my visits to Malta.

FOOD AND DRINK

Maltese cuisine has been influenced by the long relationship between the Islanders and the many invaders who occupied the Islands over the centuries. This mixture of tastes has given Malta an eclectic mix of Mediterranean cooking. Although the restaurant scene is a mix of speciality restaurants, there are many little gems that offer or specialise in local fare, serving their own versions of specialities.

Traditional Maltese food is rustic and based on the seasons. Special treats are Lampuki Pie (fish pie), Rabbit Stew, Bragioli (beef olives), Kapunata, (Maltese version of ratatouille), and widow's soup, which includes a small round of Gbejniet (sheep or goat's cheese). On most food shop counters, you'll see Bigilla, a thick pate of broad beans with garlic. The snacks that must be tried are 'hobz biz-zejt' (round of bread dipped in olive oil, rubbed with ripe tomatoes and filled with a mix of tuna, onion, garlic, tomatoes and capers) and pastizzi (flaky pastry parcel filled with ricotta or mushy peas).

A trip to the Marsaxlokk fish market on Sunday morning will show just how varied the fish catch is in Maltese waters. Depending on the season, you'll see spnotta (bass), dott (stone fish), cerna (grouper), dentici (dentex), sargu (white bream) and trill (red mullet). Swordfish and tuna follow later in the season, around early to late autumn, followed by the famed Lampuka, or dolphin fish. Octopus and squid are very often used to make some rich stews and pasta sauces.

If like me, you fancy dessert delicacies, you won't be able to resist the delicious Kannoli (tube of crispy, fried pastry filled with ricotta), Sicilian-style, semi-freddo desserts (mix of sponge, ice-cream, candied fruits and cream) and Helwa tat-Tork (sweet sugary mixture of crushed and whole almonds).

Malta may not be renowned like its larger Mediterranean neighbours for wine production, but Maltese vintages are more than holding their own at international competitions, winning several accolades in France, Italy and further afield.

International grape varieties grown on the Islands include Cabernet Sauvignon, Merlot, Syrah, Grenache, Sauvignon Blanc, Chardonnay, Carignan, Chenin Blanc and Moscato. The indigenous varieties are Gellewza and Ghirghentina, which are producing some excellent wines of distinct body and flavour.

Another Maltese winner is their very own beer, Cisk. It is my drink when on the island and I must say that in all the countries I've visited, I have not tasted a better pint of lager.

TRADITIONAL MALTESE CUISINE

Maltese food is rustic in character, full of the flavour and colour, typical of a central Mediterranean Island. The food is influenced by Malta's proximity to Sicily and North Africa but with a special slant of its own.

Traditional food is the Maltese preference. A glass of smooth local wine with friends in a village bar comes with a dish of olives, some gbejniet (local sheep's cheeses), zalzett (coriander flavoured Maltese sausage) with galletti (Maltese crackers) and some bigilla (broad bean pate) served with Maltese bread and olive oil; or on a cold day hot pastizzi (savoury ricotta filled pastries) are perfect with wine or coffee. Summer days at the beach means hobs biz-zejt, a popular snack made from a thick slice of crusty Maltese bread, rubbed with juicy, red tomatoes and topped with mint, a little onion, sheep's cheese and anchovies all soaked in delicious green olive oil; a taste of sunshine, a taste of Malta.

Summer village festivals produce sweet street foods like imqaret (date pastries) and Qubbajt (nougat) to enjoy along with the fireworks and processions. Special family meals bring on serious dishes like Ross fil-forn, (Baked Rice), Imqarrun (baked Macaroni) or Timpana (a very special rich pasta baked in a pastry case) often followed by rabbit or meat dishes served with Maltese potatoes and vegetables.

Over the last few years Mediterranean cookery in Malta has enjoyed a marked resurgence and there are a number of Maltese restaurants that serve a genuine blend of Maltese and Mediterranean cuisine. One thing is certain; the Maltese love their food, are proud of their Mediterranean cooking, and are happy to share their wonderful cuisine with the rest of the world.

The Economy of Malta

Malta is a highly industrialised, service based economy. It is classified as an advanced economy by the International Monetary Fund, is considered a high income country by the World Bank and an innovation-driven economy by the World Economic Forum. It is a member of the European Union and of the Euro Zone, having formally adopted the Euro on 1 January 2008.

Tourism in Malta is an important sector of the country's economy, contributing massively to the nation's gross domestic product (GDP). It is overseen by the Malta Tourism Authority, which in turn falls under the responsibility of the Minister for Tourism, the Environment and Culture. Malta features a number of tourism attractions encompassing elements of the island's rich history and culture, its unique landscape, its climate, as well as aquatic activities associated with the Mediterranean Sea. In addition, medical tourism has become popular in Malta in recent years, especially as a result of the government's efforts to market the practice to medical tourists in the United Kingdom.

Malta is also among the 'fastest growing' digital economies in the EU according to the latest edition of the Digital Economy and Society Index 2016. Although the percentage of Maltese people making use of the Internet is below the EU average, the percentage of ICT specialists in the workforce is above average, confirming Malta's success in attracting players in the ITC industry such as I-Gaming that is growing on the island and rely heavily on technology.

Before 1800, most Maltese were either farmers or fishermen. At that time there were very few industries apart from cotton, tobacco and shipyards. During the wars, Malta's economy flourished because of its strategic location in the Mediterranean. By the end of the Second World War, Malta lost its strategic importance and the British had to provide alternative ways of income. When Malta got its independence in 1964, economic activity was weak, but huge government efforts to start up the manufacturing and tourism industry yielded good results. Aided by agreeable international economic conditions and policies that supported foreign investment, the Maltese economy sustained fast growth right to the end of the 20th century.

Since the turn of the century Malta's economy has leaped ahead due mainly to the growth of the tourist industry. As I've already said when I first visited Malta about twelve years ago tourism was only slowly creeping forward. Since then it has walked tall and now it is sprinting ahead. Each year sees new records been broken, and this remarkable growth is forecast to continue in the years ahead. 2014 was a particularly successful year, having smashed all previous records. In that year the number of incoming tourists reached a record 1.7 million, four times the population of the islands, and was the highest when compared with other European and Mediterranean destinations.

The following table will give an interesting context to the Malta tourism figures of 2014. I'm not surprised to find that the magnetism of those lovely islands attracts such large numbers of visitors from so many countries around the globe. I suspect that like me, they come to explore, are captivated, and pledge to return again and again to enjoy more Maltese magic. Here's where they came from in 2014:

Germany 143,053

Ireland 30,722

Italy 262,631

Libya 30,770

Netherlands 44,697

Russia 34,220

Scandinavia 108,647

Spain 42,285

Switzerland 31,797

United Kingdom 487,714

USA 22,402

Other 266,395

Total tourists 1,689,809

Since I began visiting Malta, I have noticed a huge change in the infrastructure of the islands. This is due largely to membership of the EU. The road network, the coastal improvements and the restoration of public buildings and monuments has been wonderful, thanks to the massive injection of European funds and the progressive development policies of successive governments.

The economy of Malta is in excellent shape, with full employment, healthy growth in all sectors, and I suspect will soon be the envy of many other larger countries.

Malta Highlights

Valletta

Valletta, The Fortress City, "a city built by gentlemen for gentlemen" is Malta's capital city. It is a living, working city, the administrative and commercial heart of the Islands. Valletta is named after its founder, the Grand Master of the Order of St. John, Jean Parisot de la Valette. The magnificent fortress city grew on the arid rock of Mount Sceberras peninsula, which rises steeply from two deep harbours, Marsamxett and Grand Harbour. Started in 1566, Valletta was completed, with its impressive bastions, forts and cathedral, in the astonishingly short time of 15 years, even more remarkable when considering the fact that mechanical tools did not exist at the time and the whole city was built entirely by hand.

For me, Valletta is the jewel in the crown of great cities, it has enraptured me since the first day I entered through its magnificent gates, and continues to warm my heart with every step I take along its welcoming streets. Most cities around the world originate sporadically, and evolve in a haphazard jigsaw of urban sprawl, with little or no distinguishing lines to indicate where the city ends and the country begins. Not so, Valletta. It becomes clear as you enter, that here is a purpose built city, brilliantly designed in Baroque architecture, massively fortified, painstakingly embellished, and with a unique and intangible charm and character,

When the Knights of St. John arrived in Malta in 1530, this area of the peninsula was uninhabited, except for a few farmers and fishermen, some small dwellings, and perhaps a little church. But these holy men had their plans well prepared. This wonderful location, high up on a plateau, and looking down on one of the great harbours of the world, soon caught their eye, seeing it as the ideal site for a big walled and fortified city, and immediately began building it. The UNESCO World Heritage City that is Valletta today is a glorious legacy of the Knights, and a testament to their wonderful vision and devotion to excellence.

The city is busy by day, yet retains a timeless atmosphere by night, that gives the feeling that you are walking back in time. The grid of narrow streets boasts some of

Europe's finest art works, churches and palaces. Valletta is abundantly rich in sites to see and explore, intriguing historical buildings around every corner: votive statues, niches, fountains and coats of arms high up on parapets. Narrow side streets are full of tiny quaint shops and cafés, while the main streets are lined with larger international branded shops for fashion, music, jewellery and much more.

Since 1974, Malta has been an Independent Democratic Republic, and the Maltese are so proud of that status and distinction, that the main street of their capital city is named Republic Street. This famous street is the heartbeat of Valletta, the assembly point of a great cosmopolitan togetherness, visitors of all nationalities sharing an appreciation of the delights of this ancient and ornate Capital. While Valletta's main street is predominantly a shopping showcase of a myriad of international brands, it is also the location of some important attractions particularly the Grand Master's Palace, the National Museum of Archaeology, and the world renowned Cathedral of St. John.

ST JOHN'S CO-CATHEDRAL

The Co-Cathedral of St John standing in the centre of Valletta is nothing short of a gem and a must-see for any tourist. Described as the first complete example of high Baroque anywhere, it epitomises the spiritual and military role of its patrons, the Knights of Malta. I'm a regular visitor and still it never fails to astonish me. I suspect it has the same effect on thousands of other visitors, because it is one of the biggest tourist attractions in Malta. Basically, it's a sixteenth-century building with a seventeenth and eighteenth-century interior. A famous Italian artist, named Mattia Preti, dropped into Malta in 1661, and preferring it to home, stayed there. It was a stroke of luck for Malta, because his genius is etched all over Valletta, none more so than on the interior of this great cathedral.

Tourists from distant lands flock to see this ancient wonder, silence is strictly enforced, and you flash a camera at your peril. Visitors gaze in awe at the majestic high alter, and the splendour of Mr Preti's work. The church floor is no less magnificent. Covered with 400 multicoloured marble tombstones, it is the last resting place of the famous Knights that conceived and created this great city and iconic cathedral. If I could read their language, I would know their names; engraved on each tombstone. Of course, like all great institutions, there was a hierarchy. The top Knights were called Grand Masters – they were the bosses – and throughout the cathedral they are commemorated in sculptors, paintings and monuments.

You wouldn't want to be in a hurry when you visit St. John's Cathedral. To linger and absorb the artistic beauty of the myriad of side alters alone would take hours, but for me, the 'Wow' sensation is in the Oratory. Now, in the world of famous artists, the name 'Caravaggio' is legionary. He may have been a loveable rogue, shunting back and forth between Italy and Malta – depending on which police force was chasing him – but his works have for centuries been priceless treasures, revered the world over. The most famous of them all is 'The Beheading of St. John', the greatest masterpiece of its time, and here it is, in all its explicit gruesome detail, a rare privilege for all to see. Malta is famous for its churches and the Co-Cathedral of St John is the most famous of them all.

UPPER BARRAKKA GARDENS

Valletta has many other must-see features and unique attractions. Top of the list for me is the wonderful Upper Barrakka Gardens, a magical spot to spend an hour or three. It is the highest point of the city and has one of the greatest harbour views in all the world. High up on the bastions, this wonderful vantage point is a place so full of beauty, wonder, and visual adventure, that I can never leave Valletta without savouring its magic, and I know the same applies to thousands of other tourists, because it is always crowded with equally enthusiastic sightseers.

They come like me, for the wonderful view that sweeps over, not only the harbour, but the rest of Valletta, as well as the great urban sprawl that is Floriana. Directly in front, I can see the massive fortifications of Fort St. Angelo, and the three cities – jutting out like long tongues into the harbour – with the exotic names: Vittoriosa, Senglea and Cospicua. I have walked every street of these mysterious 'cities' and I can tell you, they always give me a weird feeling that I'm taking a step back in time, and a stroll through ancient history. Also straight in front of me are the massive shipyards, with their huge dry-docks and gigantic cranes, reminding me that Malta is much more than historic monuments and Baroque architecture. They have important heavy industry too, and these internationally recognised shipyards are a prime example.

Looking down beneath my balcony, I can see a saluting battery of three large nineteenth-century guns, restored and ready to fire. Every day, at the stroke of twelve, uniformed members of a heritage society ceremoniously fire the guns, and if you happen to be close by and unaware of it, the explosion and shattering bang would frighten you, but most enjoy it, and it is another unique feature of the exquisite Upper Barrakka Gardens.

THE WATERFRONT

Another sight not to be missed is the Valletta Cruise Port, or The Waterfront, as it is now called. It certainly was an inspired decision to develop this old 'Pinto Wharf' on the northern shore of the Grand Harbour into what it is to-day; an ultra-modern cruise port, accommodating thousands of tourists disembarking every week from some of the world's greatest cruise liners. It stretches about one kilometre, and the centuries old warehouses and workshops lining the shore have been transformed, and elegantly refurbished into top class restaurants, cafes and shops.

Massive liners stretch the full length of the dock, towering above and dominating everything else. Thousands of passengers disembark and sprinkle all over the immediate area. Some go on walking tours of the city, some go on luxury coaches to outlying places of interest, and some are happy to wander around, sampling the Maltese cuisine, or browsing the wonderful array of shops, no doubt purchasing some traditional Maltese glass and handmade crafts. Tourism is the life blood of Malta, and each year, they welcome almost two million visitors. That works out at five tourists for every one Maltese citizen and the 'Waterfront' has contributed hugely to those remarkable figures.

This wonderful development has already won international awards for conservation of the architectural heritage, and is also becoming a popular venue for arts and music events. It is now the main venue for the famous Malta Jazz Festival in July and an important 'Wine Fair' in August. I find it amazing how, with a bit of joined-up thinking and bold initiative, an ancient old wharf, that served the Grand Harbour for centuries, could be given this new lease of life, serving the cruising tourists of the world, and at the same time boosting substantially, this little country's finances.

OTHER CHURCHES OF VALLETTA

Our Lady of Victory Church, the smallest church in Valletta and also the oldest, is pivotal to the history of Malta. Jean Parisot De La Valette, Grand Master of the Order of Knights of Malta, built it and dedicated it to the Blessed Virgin after his victory over the Ottoman invader at the lifting of the Great Siege on the of 8th September 1565, the feast of the Nativity of the Virgin. It was built on the site where a religious ceremony was held to inaugurate the laying of the foundation stone for the new city of Valletta on 28th March 1566. A church was chosen as the first building in order to express gratitude. In fact, not only is the church dedicated to the Nativity of the Virgin, but the titular painting is situated behind the main altar, and it depicts the birth of the Blessed Virgin. Grandmaster Jean Parisot de Valette personally funded the building of the church. In 1617, the Order made 'Our Lady of Victory' its Parish Church, continuing to endow it with important monuments and paintings.

On 21st August 1568, Grand Master De Valette passed away after coming down with a fever. In line with his final wishes, he was entombed in the crypt of the church, but when St. John's Co-Cathedral was built, De Valette's remains were moved there.

This tiny church is almost 'tucked-away' around the corner from the Post Office in Castille Square and some tourists may not discover it. That would be a pity because it really is worth seeing. The artwork inside alone is worth the visit, and with the extensive and painstaking restoration work done in recent years; it will take your breath away.

CHURCH OF ST PAUL'S SHIPWRECK

This magnificent church, dedicated to the shipwreck of St Paul, is not easy to find. It is hidden away in a side street off Merchant Street and the entrance belies the sheer beauty of its interior. But the extra effort in finding it is repaid handsomely by the ornate splendour of this amazing shrine to Malta's patron saint.

The church traces its origins to 1570, was designed by Gerolamo Cassar, and completed in Dec. 1582. It was ceded to the Jesuit Fathers and a new church was started in 1639. The church's facade was rebuilt in 1885 according to the design of Nicola Zammit.

The church hosts fine artistic works, including the magnificent altarpiece by Matteo Perez d'Aleccio, and paintings by Attilio Palombi, and Giuseppe Calli. The wooden titular statue of St Paul was carved in 1659 by Melchiorre Cafà, the brother of Lorenzo Gafà, who designed the dome. The statue is paraded through the streets of Valletta on February 10th, when the annual commemoration of St Paul's Shipwreck is held. This is a national holiday in Malta and this church hosts the main ceremonies in the presence of all the dignitaries of church and state. Among the many treasures in this beautiful church are a relic of the right wrist-bone of St Paul, and part of the column on which the saint was beheaded in Rome.

THE ANGLICAN CATHEDRAL

St Paul's Pro-Cathedral has an imposing presence in Independence Square. It is built in the Neo-Classical style and its 200 ft high spire is a Valletta landmark.

When Queen Adelaide (William IV's widow and Queen Victoria's aunt) arrived in Malta for the winter of 1838-9, she was "definitely not pleased" to find facilities for Protestant worship there so inadequate. This was largely because the British had been at pains not to offend the strongly Roman Catholic population. But when the dowager queen offered to pay for a church, the government relented and provided a site.

The project was entrusted to the then Superintendent of Public Works, and the foundation stone was laid by Queen Adelaide herself in March 1839. The cathedral was designed by William Scamp (Designer of Windsor Castle) and one of the features he included was a typically English spire with a peal of six bells.

Even with its elegant pillars and pilasters, this neo-classical church contrasts sharply with the highly ornate baroque churches found in large numbers throughout Malta. It is plainer, and also brighter and airier. As a living church, it has been repaired, reorganised, and redecorated over the years, with new interior fittings added, but (for example) the original coffering of the roof can be seen in the side aisles, the original organ case remains, and the font is the one presented in 1844 by John William Bowden, a Tractarian and close friend of Newman. Church records show that the first infant to be baptised in the font was the daughter of the designer Scamp and his wife Harriet, born in April 1844 and appropriately named Adelaide. Queen Adelaide's colourful banner can be seen hanging to the right of the choir stalls and organ.

Valletta has many more beautiful churches, but the four I have described here are my favourites, mainly because of their intriguing history, pivotal importance, and their beauty and splendour.

THE GRANDMASTER'S PALACE

For any visitor to Valletta remotely interested in Malta's history, an hour spent in the Grandmaster's Palace is an intriguing experience. Dominating Palace Square, it was one of the first buildings to be built in Valletta – in 1571. The original Palazzo was designed by Gelormu Cassar but successive Grandmasters enlarged and developed the building as they deemed fit to use it as their official residence.

The Grand Master's Palace has been the administrative centre of Malta for almost three and a half centuries. The original palace was the seat of the Grand Master of the Knights of St John and later, during the British colonial period, served as the Governor's palace. Today it serves as the office of the President of the Republic of Malta.

When not hosting functions of state, the magnificent halls at first floor are open to the public. The Council Chamber is home to a rare collection of exotic Gobelin tapestries depicting hunting scenes from different continents. The State Dining Room is adorned with portraits of the Presidents of Malta and one painting of Queen Elizabeth II as Queen of Malta. The Supreme Council Hall is decorated with a cycle of twelve frescoes by Mattia Perez d'Aleccio depicting the Great Siege of 1565. The Ambassador's Hall and main corridors are lined with portraits of European monarchs and Grand Masters of the Order.

The Palace Armoury is also located here and its bewildering array of armour and weaponry is nothing short of astonishing. This collection (5000 items) provides a human context to the Great Siege of Malta and the military prowess of the Knights of St John. Highlights include the personal armour of Grand Master La Valette, the dazzling parade armour of Grand Master Alof de Wignacourt, and a collection of weapons used by the Ottomans during the Great Siege of 1565.

Although I am a pacifist by nature I am always captivated by this vast display of historic military hardware. It serves to reinforce my belief that the Knights of Malta were an eminent military force and their presence in Malta was pivotal to the Islands survival.

CASA ROCCA PICCOLA

Casa Rocca Piccola is a 16th century palace situated at 74 Republic St. Valletta. It is a wonderful opportunity for tourists in the capital city to sample a taste of ancient nobility with a visit to this aristocratic and functioning residence. The palace remains the home of the noble de Piro family and has been occupied by a long line of noble tenants down through the centuries.

The Palace originally formed part of a palazzo constructed in 1580 for Don Pietro La Rocca, an Italian admiral of the Order of the Knights of St John, and its maze of rooms are a journey through privileged life on the island over the last 4 centuries. Among the diverse spaces to be seen are the Chapel, a Summer Dining Room with views over a secluded garden, the Library, and also some underground bomb shelters that sadly became necessary during World War II.

Among the vast collection of rare and finely crafted furniture is a wooden chest believed to be the oldest extant example of Maltese furniture. In the Palace's rich collection you will also see the silver surgical instruments that the Knights of St. John used in their precocious surgical techniques. Other enjoyable exhibits include a chess set from the period of the Knights, paintings by Mattia Preti and examples of Tal-Lira clocks, traditional and highly-decorated Maltese timepieces.

This is a charming, and still 'lived-in' palace in central Valletta with a treasure-trove of antiques and artworks and is well worth a visit. There are daily tours and the palace includes a restaurant and a souvenir shop.

NATIONAL MUSEUM OF FINE ARTS

The National Museum of Fine Arts presents a wonderful overview of art and artistic expression in Malta from the medieval period to the contemporary. It is set in a building that is an 18th century Italianate style palace built on the spot of one of the earliest buildings constructed in Valletta shortly after its foundation in 1566. Through the centuries it has served as a residence to successive Knights of the Order of St. John. It also hosted high-ranking personalities both as residents and guests. These include Lord Mountbatten of Burma, British Prime Minister Winston Churchill, King George V and Queen Elizabeth of England. The palace was officially inaugurated as the National Museum of Fine Arts in 1974 and has since been Malta's most important museum for the arts. The architecture of the building is an important example of the mid-eighteenth century late baroque style in Malta boasting one of the finest main staircases to be seen on the island.

Highlights from the collection on display include paintings by leading local and internationally acclaimed artists, precious Maltese silverware, statuary in marble bronze and wood, fine furniture items and splendid maiolica pieces.

Two halls are devoted to the work of Malta-based artist Mattia Preti, who painted the vaulted ceilings of St. John's Co-Cathedral. The Italian-born Baroque master is in good company, such as famed British artist Turner, whose sole depiction of Malta, an exquisite watercolour of the Grand Harbour, is on display at the museum. Other exhibited work includes the varied output of contemporary Maltese artists such as sculptor Antonio Sciortino.

For lovers of fine art, this museum, small by international standards, tucked away in one of Valletta's back streets will be an absolute delight. It is well worth a visit, not only for the small Turner alone, but for the magical Mattia Preti exhibition, and for all the other varied and enchanting objects of priceless art.

MANOEL THEATRE

One of the oldest working theatres in the world, the Manoel Theatre, is located in Old Theatre Street in the heart of Valletta. It was built in 1732 by Grand Master Antonio Manoel de Vilhena and is rightly considered a magnificent jewel in the capital city's crown. A 623 seat venue with an oval-shaped auditorium and tiers of boxes, the theatre is home to the brilliant Malta Philharmonic Orchestra. With the boxes made of wood and adorned with 22-carat gold lead and a shade of pale blue, the interior has underwent a number of alterations whilst still retaining its original features such as the white Carrara marble staircase and impressive chandeliers.

The theatre is a baroque gem with a wonderful acoustic environment. Today it stages everything from contemporary plays to opera and attracts performers from all around the world. As an active participant in promoting local talent in drama, the theatre also invites Maltese opera singers to collaborate with foreign performers in the Opera Festival every March.

During the Second World War, the Manoel Theatre managed to escape any serious damage. It served as a shelter for the homeless and victims of the bombings during that prolonged siege and provided a welcome refuge for the beleaguered and war weary Maltese.

Many visitors to Valletta, lucky like me to have discovered this architectural gem, take a tour around the fascinating, historic and spectacular theatre. Guided tours of the theatre and its museum are conducted daily. Lavish stage costumes are on display at the museum, along with antique sound-effects machines and archival programmes. This tour will take you through the theatre itself as well as the attached museum which covers much of the fascinating history of the Manoel Theatre. It is well worth the modest entry fee and the audio guide gives you an insight into both the history of the building and the cultural life of Malta.

THE MALTA EXPERIENCE

This wonderful tourist attraction is undoubtedly the best of Malta's many visual shows, providing an entertaining general introduction to the island's history and culture. Sensational vision and a gripping commentary tell the story of 7000 years of island history in a purpose-built auditorium in Valletta, overlooking the magnificent Grand Harbour. The narration is available in a choice of 16 languages and the show is continuously updated in both content and technology to ensure it stays up-to-the-minute.

With its beautiful imagery and atmospheric sound, The Malta Experience enriches our appreciation of the island's people and places. It gives a much deeper understanding of the history to be found in Malta's many magnificent landmarks, such as the ancient prehistoric temples of stone-age settlers, the old world silent city of Mdina and the majestic fortressed walls of Valletta.

The show is educational, informative and entertaining, and gives a great overview of the character of the Maltese Islands. Although many visitors will have read about Malta in guide books or on the Internet, this presentation is the perfect first stop on a cultural and historical tour of the islands.

FORT ST ELMO

Guarding the entrance to both Marsamxett and Grand Harbours is Fort St Elmo, named after the patron saint of mariners. This iconic landmark is located at the far end of Republic Street and is the fort that bore the brunt of Turkish arms during the Great Siege of 1565. In 1552, four Italian architects were commissioned to begin construction of the fort and from the sixteenth to the twentieth century, a number of expansions and renovations were made, adding Italian, French, Spanish, and British influence to the original structure. The result is a 50,400-square-meter complex with intimidating defence walls, upper and lower parade grounds, arsenals, a chapel and storage houses. Having endured many sieges, the fort is now part of the larger harbour fortification complex. Fort St. Elmo is a monument to Maltese cultural, historical, and military engineering heritage. After restoration and renovation the fort opened to the public in 2015 containing the amazing National War Museum.

The National War Museum, located in the Lower St. Elmo, is one of the top places of interest and amongst the most popular museums in Malta. It provides visitors with a good insight into what Malta went through during the two World Wars. This War Museum represents the important role the Maltese people played during World War II as well as Malta's important military role after 1800 under British rule. The museum also displays items from the First World War and from the two years of French Occupation. The National War Museum in Malta opened in 1975 and was completely refurbished in 2009. It consists of a large vaulted hall, two long annexes, one on each side of the hall and three smaller rooms. The left annex is largely dedicated to the Royal Navy with various uniforms, equipment, emblems, Malta convoys and several other related items on display.

The large main hall has several important items on show such as the Italian E-Boat, anti-aircraft guns, the Willis Jeep 'Husky' that General Eisenhower used during his visit to Malta', the famous Gloster Gladiator 'Faith', the George Cross, the Book of Remembrance, the illuminated Scroll presented by President Franklin D. Roosevelt and wreckage of a Spitfire and a Messerschmitt Me-109 fighter aircraft recovered from the sea bed.

The photographic exhibition is also worth examining as it illustrates the extremely harsh conditions that Malta and its people had to go through during the war. The images show the great deal of damage that was caused to Malta and the areas that had to be rebuilt. Other interesting features are the prestigious awards and decorations received by Maltese service men and civilians during World War II for their bravery and sacrifice that helped Malta survive the war. For me, the most important and interesting piece at the War Museum is the George Cross Medal which King George presented in 1942 to the whole population of Malta as a recognition of their bravery during the war and which now features on the national flag.

THE THREE CITIES

Surrounding the Grand Harbour in the South of Malta, directly opposite Valletta, the three walled towns known as the 'Three Cities,' Vittoriosa, Cospicua and Senglea, offer a fascinating glimpse into Malta's maritime history. The original home of the Knights of St John, the 'Three Cities' have jutted out into the Grand Harbour since Phoenician times. Predominantly maritime cities, they have been doorways to commerce, migration, encounters and cultural exchange in Malta's long history.

With the development of the shipbuilding and shipping industries at nearby Marsa, dockyard workers set up homes in the 'Three Cities,' but during World War 11 they suffered severe bombing raids with Cospicua and Senglea being extensively damaged. Today the 'cities' atmosphere is captivating, with the people living within the city walls immensely proud of their heritage. Each town comes with its own particular magnetism and character that distinguishes them from other localities on the island and it could be said that with their beautiful churches, grandiose palaces and imposing bastions, the 'Three Cities' history is arguably as rich as that of Malta's capital, Valletta.

This historical area has been left rather unexplored by tourists and it has largely retained its past architectural glory (even though very heavily hit during World War II). Having claimed its rightful place in Malta's expansive history, the region has been undergoing a revival in popularity in recent years. 'The Three Cities' are now brimming with exclusive restaurants, wine bars, museums and a yacht marina, making them very attractive places to wander and explore.

The 'Three Cities' are enclosed by the Cottonera Lines, along with several other fortifications. The term Cottonera is synonymous with the 'Three Cities,' although it is sometimes taken to also include the nearby town of Kalkara. Together, the 'Three Cities' have a total population of 11,000 people.

Vittoriosa is an intriguing place to visit. I always get great pleasure just strolling around the tidy narrow streets which are lovingly embellished by the residents who are so proud of their ancient 'city.' This little town has the distinction of having been chosen by the Knights of St John when they required an alternative governing location to the old city of Mdina to give them a better watch over their fleets. It was just a small village then called Birgu, but the Knights expanded and fortified it, and when in 1565 they defeated the massive invasion of Turks from this fortified base, they renamed it Vittoriosa, meaning Victorious City.

Today, the city walls and the buildings within Vittoriosa are full of mystery and intrigue. When wandering within the city walls, I see plaques which indicate their historical importance to curious explorers. I love to visit one or more of the several museums, of which the notable Inquisitor's Palace is the most impressive. The Maritime museum is also fascinating with fine examples of model ships, paintings, nautical instruments, weapons and traditional Maltese boats.

The 'city' has its own little modern commercial area, adjacent to the yacht marina, known as the Vittoriosa Waterfront. Here there are some quality restaurants, cafes and a casino. The town's narrow streets also have some lovely Dine and Wine bars with unique atmosphere and plenty of old world character.

Cospicua or Bormla (its original name), is full of culture and history. A walk around this ancient little town will allow you to admire and appreciate its distinct character and old world charm. Some buildings still bear the scars of the bombing during the Second World War, and you can identify the newer parts which had to be completely rebuilt.

In Cospicua, the Dockyard Creek remains prominent. Even the Phoenicians took refuge for their ships here. Later the Carthaginians and the Romans continued to exploit the facilities of the Grand Harbour, one of the largest natural harbours in the world. Cospicua's location, between the promontories of Vittoriosa and Senglea, have dictated its purpose and made its place in history.

Senglea, (originally named L-Isla) like most of the walled cities of Malta, has a proud and colourful legacy in the turbulent history of Malta. So quiet and peaceful now, it is hard to imagine that the whole of this little town had been bombed to rubble during the Second World War and had to be almost completely rebuilt. The reason for this harsh bombardment lay in the fact that the wharves beneath the bastions of Isla had been converted into a Naval Dockyard by the British, who enlarged and developed the shipyard that was originally started by the Knights of the Order of St John. The Malta Shipyard in Senglea has for long held a proud reputation in the entire Mediterranean region and commands the importance of the Grand Harbour of Malta.

Several streets in Senglea have steps which lead down to its most stunning area, the waterfront and the marina. My favourite spot is the tip of the peninsula where I can enjoy the gardens and the wonderful views of the harbour from the famous Gardjola (pronounced Gardyola), a decorated watch-tower or vedette that has become a much admired Maltese icon. The 'Three Cities' offer an intriguing insight into Malta and its history. Their harbour inlets have been in use since Phoenician times: the docks always providing a living for local people, but also leaving them vulnerable when Malta's rulers were at war. As the first home to the Knights of St. John, the 'Three Cities' palaces, churches, forts and bastions are far older than Valletta's. For me, this is the heart of Malta, where the spirit, courage and endurance of the Maltese people were severely tested throughout the centuries, but where their character, bravery and resilience always shone through.

When I stroll around those hallowed narrow streets I can almost hear the bombs and artillery and feel a sense of awe and wonder to be in this place of such glorious history and in the presence of such a unique community.

THE INQUISITOR'S PALACE

The Inquisitor's Palace is located in the beautiful and historic town of Vittoriosa in one of its small, narrow and winding streets. It was built in 1530 and is now the only Inquisitor's Place open to the public in the whole world, as many of the other palaces were destroyed during the French Revolution.

Mgr Pietro Dusina, who was the first general inquisitor residing in the palace back in 1574 and the inquisitors after him strived to transform the palace into a typical and beautiful Roman palace. Over the years, the palace was used as a hospital, mess house and a refugee camp. It is now home to the museum of Ethnography which has an interesting and rare collection on display, focusing on the urban religious culture in Malta and religious values hidden in Maltese identity and culture to the present day.

The museum focuses on the impact of the inquisition on the Maltese society through the centuries. The Inquisitor's Palace also has a lovely central courtyard on the ground floor, prison cells, waiting room, audience hall and several other beautiful and interesting rooms, several of them already restored and open to visitors.

Although the purpose and use of the Inquisitor's Palaces around the world reminds us of dark days and brutal practises which I abhor, thankfully, they are now ancient history. However a visit to this last remaining one, restored and intact, is interesting, intriguing and informative.

ST LAWRENCE'S CHURCH

The jewel of Vittoriosa's waterfront is undoubtedly the beautiful church of St Lawrence, a 17th century reconstruction of the original church built by the Knights of St John in 1530. It is an imposing landmark with a magnificent dome and twin clock towers. The interior of this historic parish church is lavishly decorated with a unique collection of priceless treasures including the wonderful painting, 'The Martyrdom of St Lawrence,' by Malta's greatest artist, Mattia Preti.

In 1941, as World War 11 was raging and Malta was suffering severe bombing raids, the arrival of the aircraft carrier HMS 'Illustrious' into the Grand Harbour was a welcome sight for the war weary Maltese. Many believed the war was coming to an end. But it soon became apparent that the ship had suffered severe damage and loss of life. The aircraft carrier was hit six times while escorting a convoy in the Sicily channel and was hit a seventh time in another attack as it approached Malta.

Despite the savage attack it suffered, and having been hit by more bombs than any other carrier, HMS 'Illustrious' managed to contain its fires, stem the flooding and limp into the relative safety of the Grand Harbour on January 10, 1941. The loss, however, was tragic: 126 crew members had been killed and 91 injured.

The presence of this famous enemy ship in the shelter of Malta's Grand Harbour didn't deter the German Luftwaffe and soon the first dive-bombing raids began with their menacing Junkers 88 and 89, so brutal and devastating that they reduced the inner harbour area, particularly Senglea and Vittoriosa, to a vast heap of ruins.

On January 16th, 1941 the Church of St Lawrence was bombed by a German air raid. Both the sacristy and the chapter hall were destroyed. Thirty-three civilians, who were sheltering in the sacristy, were buried under the mass of rubble. The parish priest, who was sheltering in the belfry tower, dazed and badly shaken, rushed to the scene giving the last rites and helping the rescue efforts. The bodies were subsequently recovered from underneath the debris and miraculously, there was one survivor, a young baby. On March 22nd of the same year the chapel of the Blessed Sacrament was destroyed and on April 4th 1942, the dome of the church was destroyed. The chapel was re-built in 1951 and the dome was re-built in 1952. A visit to this beautiful, peaceful church today brings me back to those awful days of war horror and I say a silent prayer in gratitude for the peace we now enjoy and in memory of all the victims who gave their lives in those tragic events.

OUR LADY OF VICTORIES CHURCH

In a lovely square in Senglea stands the beautiful church of Our Lady of Victories. It is so named to commemorate Malta's famous victory in The Great Siege of 1565. During World War 11, this church was also destroyed by the Germans because it obstructed the aircraft from dive bombing the dockyards. After the war the church was completely rebuilt and restored to its former glory as a beautiful shrine in honour of Our Lady.

This church is now a place of pilgrimage because of its famous statue of 'Kristu Redentur,' which is believed to have miraculous healing powers. It is an amazing depiction of Christ collapsing under the cross and it rests in a red-velvet niche in a side chapel to the right of the main alter. A growing stream of pilgrims visit the shrine each day to pray for divine healing, and having prayed there myself many times, I have to say that I am always happy to have come.

Mdina

The Silent City

Mdina is a tiny medieval city enclosed in bastions, located on a large hilltop in the centre of Malta. It was the old capital city of Malta and with its narrow streets, few inhabitants and beautiful views over the island; it is truly a magical place to visit. Behind its fortified walls, Mdina's timeless beauty has been captivating nobilities throughout its 4000 years of existence.

In medieval times Mdina was called Città Notabile – the Noble City. It was the favoured residence of the Maltese aristocracy and the seat of the Università (governing council). It has been home to Malta's many noble families, some of which are descendants of the Norman,

Sicilian and Spanish overlords who have made Mdina their home in centuries past. The Knights of St John, who were largely a sea-based force, made the Grand Harbour and Valletta their centre of activity, and Mdina gradually receded into the background as a holiday destination for the nobility. Today it is home to around 300 people who live within the city walls. In contrast, the town of Rabat, a short distance away has a population of over 11000 people.

It was the Normans who surrounded the city of Mdina with its thick defensive fortifications and they also widened the moat surrounding the city. After an earthquake in 1693, when serious damage was done, there was the need to redesign parts of the city. This introduced Baroque designs, and the Knights of Malta rebuilt the cathedral as well as the Magisterial Palace and Palazzo Falzon.

Today, with its massive walls and peaceful, shady streets, Mdina is often referred to as the Silent City, a nickname that becomes very appropriate after dark. With narrow, cobbled streets shrouded in an air of mystery, it is always a scene of fascination and intrigue for me. The historic citadel and ancient capital is one of Malta's most beautiful spots. Perched so high, it can be seen from every corner of the island. As I enter through the massive gate and meander around this mysterious golden-stone Arabic walled city I feel a sense of strange spiritualism and although I sometimes wonder if I may be trespassing or disturbing the slumber of an old ghost town, the magnetism of its enchantment keeps me going.

I can spend many relaxing hours in this old world city, now resting in retirement, but once a hive of activity as the important seat of government. Its main function now is to welcome and charm visitors like me to its beautiful palaces, museums and churches, especially St Paul's Cathedral, outstanding for its renowned baroque architecture. Malta's old capital is the island's most perfectly preserved medieval treasure. The peace and tranquillity is a joy to behold and along its quiet narrow streets and alleyways you can almost touch the sense of history.

For tourists from all over the world, Mdina is a must-see attraction. It's got everything, history, culture, panoramic views, stunning architecture, palaces, churches, quaint narrow streets opening to lovely little courtyards offering amazing photo opportunities and lots of little restaurants/tea rooms should you want a break as well as little shops offering the beautiful Mdina glass. Not to be missed!

Mdina Treasures

ST PAUL'S CATHEDRAL

St Pauls Cathedral, dominating the heart of Mdina is an architectural gem built in the 17th century to replace a Norman cathedral that had been destroyed by the earthquake in 1693. According to the Book of Acts, Paul and his missionary party were shipwrecked on Malta for three months. During his stay, Paul was bitten by a snake and remained unharmed, prompting the natives to regard him as a god. He later healed the father of the governor of the island, Publius, and many other people (Acts 27:1-11). According to tradition, Publius was converted to Christianity and went on to become the bishop of Malta and later of Athens. St. Paul's Cathedral stands on the traditional site of Publius' town house and headquarters. The new cathedral took five years to build and caused a significant redesign of medieval Mdina's city centre; several streets and houses were cleared to create an open square in front of the cathedral.

St. Paul's Cathedral is a unique masterpiece, designed by architect Lorenzo Gafa. Its impressive façade wows visitors as they emerge from Mdina's narrow streets. The cathedral's magnificent dome, with red-and-white stripes, dominates the skyline. The dome's interior has been decorated by a succession of painters; today's decoration dates from the 1950s.

The lavish interior of the cathedral is similar in many ways to the Cathedral of St. John in Valetta. There are great works by the famous artist and knight, Mattia Preti, and a marble inlaid floor with tombstones carrying the coats of arms and inscriptions of the bishops of Mdina and other members of the cathedral chapter.

Surviving from the original Norman church is a monumental depiction of the conversion of St. Paul by Mattia Preti, between the apse and main altar. Also surviving from the old church are the 15th-century Tuscan panel painting of the Madonna and Child, the baptismal font, the frescoes in the apse depicting St. Paul's shipwreck, and the 900-year-old portal, made of carved Irish bog wood, which now serves as a door to the vestry.

In my opinion, this magnificent church is second only to St John's Co-Cathedral in Valletta for its majesty and splendour. The wonderful baroque architecture, the perfect location and setting, and the grandeur of its interior is a special treat for me and for tourists from all over the world who come every day, gaze in awe, and leave enraptured by the experience.

CATHEDRAL MUSEUM

Located in a splendid 18th century baroque palace, the Cathedral Museum contains a wonderful collection of art works, many by famous Old Masters, The museum was once a seminary built by bishop Paolo Alpheran de Bussan (1728-1757) and is considered as one of the best church museums in Europe, fully deserving the appellation of Crossroad of Faith and Culture.

The museum traces its origins to a fabulous donation made by Marquis Saverio Marchesi, who decreed, in his last will, that once his family became extinct, all the artistic works the family possessed were to be given to the Cathedral Chapter. This came about in 1896. The idea of turning some halls adjacent to the Cathedral into a museum matured during the 1960s. Displaying tapestries and liturgical vestments from St. John Cathedral, the old Mdina Seminary was officially opened and renamed the Mdina Cathedral Museum in 1969.

The eclectic and rich treasure trove of historical artefacts, includes engravings by Rembrandt, woodcuts and copperplates by Albrecht Durer, archived documents from the Inquisition, a rare coin collection spanning 2000 years, a set of 15 Silver and Gold statues of the Apostles, and a silver collection bequeathed to the Cathedral

Museum by Dr Jimmy Farrugia, former Speaker of Malta's House of Representatives.

A visit to this stunning museum following a breathtaking tour of the Cathedral is an amazing treat for art lovers and will undoubtedly be the highlight of your trip to the Silent City of Mdina.

THE MDINA DUNGEONS

Situated beside the main entrance gate, just inside the great walls of the Silent City is the Mdina Dungeon Museum. It is located underneath the Vilhena Palace and in olden times it was actually used as a prison.

The dungeons comprise a series of underground passageways and chambers which portray the "dark side" of Malta history and visitors can explore and wander around at leisure. Here the various types of torture which was practised in Malta in its ancient past are recreated using lifelike waxwork figures. The histories covered in this museum represent the Roman, the Knights of Malta and the Arab periods.

This is gory stuff. The scenes recreated are gruesome, as you would expect from torture chambers, but the intriguing aspect of it is the fact that a lot of the acts of torture which are depicted in these chambers actually took place in these same rooms and cells. During the Roman period, the Maltese Islands were used as a slave colony and in those times, crucifixion, torture and beheading were very common. During the Arab period, a common form of torture was to crush the victims beneath very large stones. The Knights of St. John also brought many brutal torture methods.

When the Office of the Inquisitor was established in 1561 to suppress heresy among Catholics, some hideous forms of torture were used in that suppression. Likewise during the French occupation period, torture and brutality was practised. These are all depicted in the Dungeon Museum in all their gruesome detail.

For some, this can be fascinating and entertaining. I have to admit that one visit to view the recreations of those gory days was more than enough for me. But for those who wish to see re-enactments of this dark and ancient history; feel free. It is another hidden part of Mdina, The Silent City.

Rabat

The historic town of Rabat located within a ten minute walk from Mdina is the next stop for tourists after their visit to the Silent City. In fact the two were one city in Roman times and since being separated by the Arab-built walls around Mdina, Rabat has progressed and flourished as a charming old world town and also a lively business and commercial centre. Founded in the Middle Ages it is now a major Maltese town with a population of 11,500 inhabitants.

The town is a commercial hub for central Malta and acts as a market to its large agricultural hinterland. It is also well established on the tourist map due to its archaeological and historical sites: The Roman Villa (Domus Romana), catacombs, St. Paul's Grotto and the fine churches and monasteries.

Rabat has also played an important role in Malta's history. For many centuries, religious orders have established themselves within the town and Franciscans, Dominicans and Augustinians still flourish here in their large convents and monasteries, catering for the religious needs of parishioners in their churches.

Rabat is home to one of the most sacred places in Malta, Saint Paul's Grotto. This is a small and intimate cave where, according to tradition, St Paul spent a few months after his shipwreck on the island. This underground grotto is revered not only in Malta but worldwide. Pope John Paul visited the shrine in 1990 and it is a special attraction for a constant stream of pilgrims and one of the highlights of a visit to Rabat.

Above the grotto there is an impressive building with a magnificent baroque facade. The building encompasses two churches: the Collegiate Church of St Paul and the small church of St Publius. Both churches contain works by Preti. For the Church of St Publius, Grand Master Carafa commissioned from Preti a painting of the Virgin with Child and the Saints John the Baptist and Publius. These works symbolise the link between St Paul's Grotto, Malta's Christian origins and the Order of the Knights. For the church of St Paul, Preti created the Martyrdom of St Stephen and St Michael Archangel. Other works by Preti in Rabat can be seen in the Church of St Mark, in the Wignacourt Museum and in Verdala Palace, the summer residence of the Grand Masters in the past, and of the President of Malta today.

CATACOMBS OF ST PAUL AND ST AGATHA

Rabat is the location of the oldest and largest evidence of Christianity on the Maltese islands. St. Paul's Catacombs, an archaeological treasure and a typical complex of adjoined underground Roman cemeteries, were unearthed in the town in 1894.

The site consists of more than thirty hypogeal over two large areas. The main one covers an area of more than 2000 square meters of interconnecting passages and tombs. St. Paul's Catacombs were named as such due to the myth that they were also once linked to St. Paul's Grotto. Much larger examples of Roman catacombs may be found in Rome but the uniqueness of these subterranean cemeteries lies in their unique showcase of Maltese underground architecture. An intriguing feature of the catacombs is the circular agape tables, which were carved out of the rock so that the relatives of the dead could assemble underground for ritual funeral and anniversary feasts with their departed loved ones.

The Saint Paul's Catacombs complex houses a very small collection of artefacts that is directly related to funerary practices of Imperial and Late Roman periods. Unfortunately very little is known about the material found within the tombs of this complex but artefacts found in other burial complexes in Malta show that the material remains buried with the deceased were often of similar types. These artefacts include decorated lamps, unguentarii and balsamarii, copper bracelet and bone pins, figurines and funerary inscriptions.

The St Paul and St Agatha's Catacombs, now in the care of Heritage Malta, are situated in lovely surroundings, among trees and shrubs. The small museum at the entrance displays a varied and interesting collection ranging from coins to Roman, Etruscan and Egyptian artefacts. A visit to this medieval treasure is surely a highlight of any tourist's stay in Malta. It certainly was intriguing and fascinating for me and I look forward to more visits to further explore those hidden treasures.

VERDALA PALACE AND BUSKETT GARDENS

The Verdala Palace is perched on a hilltop adjoining and overlooking Buskett Gardens in a lush valley south of Rabat and east of Dingli. It was built by Grand Master Hughes de Verdalle in 1588 as a summer residence. The palace is not open to the public, but it does offer a notable landmark visible clearly from Dingli Cliffs, towering as it does over the Buskett woodland.

The site of Verdala Palace was originally occupied by a hunting lodge, which was built in the 1550s or 1560s during the reign of Grand Master Jean Parisot de Valette. The lodge was built in the *Boschetto*, a large semi-landscaped area that was used by the Knights of the Order of St John for game hunting. The hunting lodge was expanded into a palace in 1586, during the reign of Hugues Loubenx de Verdalle and was further embellished in the 17th and 18th centuries.

The palace then became the Governor's country residence and in the Second World War was used as a repository for the National Museum of Arts. Later it played host to many distinguished dignitaries including King George and Queen Mary, King George VII, King Edward VII and Queen Alexandra, Colonel Gaddafi of Libya, Josip Broz Tito of Yugoslavia and President Leone of Italy.

Verdala Palace was designed by the famous Maltese architect, Glormu Cassar, who designed many other iconic buildings including St John's Co-Cathedral in Valletta. With four towers, one on each corner, this is another impressive example of Cassar's wonderful creativity and is well worth seeing. It is now the official summer residence of the President of Malta and is not open to the public. In recent years some important fund raising events including the annual August Moon Ball and concerts in aid of the President's Community Chest Fund are held at the palace.

Just west of Verdala Palace are the beautiful Buskett Gardens, a wooded area created in the 17th century and is an extension to the palace gardens. It is Malta's only surviving mature woodland, a dense collection of oaks, olives, orange, cactus, pines, cypress trees, shrubs and flowers. The lush gardens provide a peaceful, relaxing haven for locals and visitors and are a popular place for picnics and for nature lovers exploring the flora and fauna.

The gardens are very popular with the Maltese people, and serve as a venue for the festival on the Feast of Imnarja which is celebrated each year on 29th June. Hundreds of people flock there the previous evening, to eat the traditional Maltese dish of rabbit stew cooked in wine, to listen to traditional folk music and singing, and to enjoy the annual agricultural show in the morning. The gardens can be explored by following several peaceful pathways, are greenest from autumn to spring with a lot of wild flowers and natural springs, and in summer the trees offer cooling shade from the hot sun. I always find that my stroll around Verdala Palace and Buskett Gardens on a lovely warm day is both refreshing and relaxing and great sustenance for body and soul.

DINGLI CLIFFS

Dingli is a village near the western coastline of Malta, with a population of around 3,600. It is two kilometres from Rabat and it lies on a plateau some 250 metres above sea level, which is one of the highest points of Malta. The area provides not only open sea views over the tiny, uninhabited isle of Filfla, but is also a good vantage point over Malta. From the cliffs there are also views of the nearby Buskett Gardens and Verdala Palace. The name *Dingli* is believed to be derived from the name of Sir Thomas Dingley, an English Knight of the Order of St. John, who owned much of the lands in the surrounding area. Nearby are the spectacular Dingli Cliffs, the highest spot on the island and the most fantastic sea views in Malta. Their flat rocky top is a great place for walking and there is usually a beautiful refreshing breeze up there. It is also possible to drive along the edge of the cliff for some distance.

The views of the Mediterranean are spectacular and this is a popular spot from which to watch the sunset. In spring the area is covered in wild flowers, in summer wild fennel and caper bushes flourish, and the smell of thyme wafts up as you brush the greenery underfoot. The cliffs are simply majestic, particularly if viewed from a boat while cruising, but also from the top - the views are breathtaking, overlooking the small terraced fields below, the open sea, and Filfla, the small uninhabited island just across.

It is also a place to unearth important local history and archaeology. Here we find the most impressive concentration of 'Cart Ruts' in Malta. Those 'Ruts', burrowed into the rocks, have been a mystery to archaeologists, striving to find a satisfactory explanation as to their origin. The most accepted theory is that they were made by cart wheels during the Bronze Age (2300-800 BC). British archaeologists have named this network of 'Ruts' found in Dingli, 'Clapham Junction Cart Ruts' after a similar intricate network of rail lines at Clapham Junction station in South London.

This area of Malta has long been one of my favourites. This is where land and sea collide and where untamed beauty abounds. I love to drive around this heavenly landscape at my leisure. The panoramic views over the deep blue Mediterranean always takes my breath away. The peaceful rural life of the surrounding countryside is a soothing experience to savour and if I'm lucky I might even spot a goat herder sitting in a field watching his flock graze in the lush winter grass or I might meet up with the last shepherd roaming the cliffs.

THE BLUE GROTTO

The Blue Grotto is one of a number of sea caverns on the west coast of Malta, beside the quaint little villages of Qrendi and Zurrieq, overlooking the sheer cliffs of the rugged western coastline. Just across is the small islet of Filfla, which is uninhabited but is now a bird sanctuary. It is one of the most visited beauty spots on Malta because of its idyllic location, its mesmerising clear waters and the brilliant blue and emerald light flooding into the Blue Grotto cave.

Every day from sunrise until about 1 pm a unique sight can be observed here. The location of the caves combined with the sunlight leads to the water mirroring, showing numerous shades of blue. Several caverns mirror the brilliant phosphorescent colours of the underwater flora; other caverns show a deep dark shade of blue. There are six caves in all and the best way to view those intriguing caves and surrounding cliffs is to take the short boat trip that is available in the little harbour.

The 25 minute trip takes you into the Blue Grotto, which is about 30 metres high and in through the other caves. I have had this amazing experience and for me, the most fascinating aspect was the spectrum of shades of blue that the sea absorbs, depending on the light entering the caves and its reflection from the seabed. The beautiful turquoise shades contrasts sharply with the coral colours of the surrounding rocks.

The Blue Grotto is one of the most popular destinations for tourists on the island of Malta and throughout the year it is busy welcoming scores of coaches, ferrying visitors to this must-see attraction. Scuba diving, snorkelling and rock climbing are also very popular activities here. It also has some typical local restaurants that offer good food with stunning views. This unique and beautiful location has been used many times by filmmakers, including a scene of the 2004 film 'Troy.'

The best time of the year to visit the Blue Grotto is in the spring or autumn as the site can get extremely busy during summer. To enjoy the caves at their best, it is better to go early in the morning when the sun is lower in the sky and the sea is calmer. In case that the water may be too rough, or you don't have enough time for a boat trip, there is a viewing platform on the road leading to site, where you can also enjoy this unique natural wonder.

HAGAR QIM AND MNAJDRA TEMPLES

The temple of Hagar Qim has stood on a hilltop overlooking the sea and the island of Filfla for over 5000 years since 3600-3200 BC. A short distance away is the temple of Mnajdra and the forecourt and facade of both follow the typical pattern of other temples across the islands. These two adjacent temple complexes are among the most evocative prehistoric monuments on Malta.

Hagar Qim and its layout is the least understood of all the temples on the Maltese Islands. It comprises four temples and two entrances, one at the front and one at the rear. It was an imposing circular structure high on a plateau which made it clearly visible over a wide distance. The impressive facade of the front entrance and the giant standing slabs that still survive, indicate its original grandeur. The temple is a complex of spaces and chambers adjoining each other in an intricate maze of rooms and the understanding of these designs has still not become clear after all those centuries.

The most important relics discovered here were a number of 'Fat Lady' figurines of naked women dubbed by archaeologists 'Venus' of Malta' and now exhibited in the National Museum of Archaeology in Valletta. This would indicate the temple was a fertility shrine dedicated to Mother Earth and perhaps it was believed that the dead would only return to her womb if sacrifices were made in these holy places. Historians are convinced that offerings of animals' blood and milk were certainly made in both temples.

Mnajdra consists of three temples known as South, Middle and East, facing a common oval forecourt. It also dates from 3600 – 3200 BC. The layout of its continuous concave facade arranged in an arena-like design would suggest that this is where the congregation gathered with the priests conducting the ceremonies inside. Thanks to its good state of preservation and spectacular location, Mnajdra is the most atmospheric of Malta's many ancient temples. Opposite the main entrance is the doorway to a set of apses flanked by two large blocks decorated with small drilled holes. This doorway and the decorated blocks mark the position of the rising sun on the first day of spring and autumn (the Equinoxes) and the first day of summer and winter (the Solstices). The temples are opened to the public at sunrise on the spring equinox to allow visitors to view the impressive event.

Artifacts found at Mnajdra include stone and clay statuettes, shell and stone ornaments, flint tools and decorated earthenware. The lack of any metal objects is one of the indications of its Neolithic origin. The temples are a UNESCO World Heritage Site, inscribed as part of

'The Megalithic Temples of Malta' in the World Heritage List. They are "an outstanding example of a type of building which illustrates a significant stage in human history". A dedicated visitor centre offers full information about the site in a fun and interactive manner.

This is a magical part of Malta. I call it 'The Wild Mediterranean Way.' Where in the world would one get such natural beauty, idyllic seascapes, amazing caves and rock formation, spectacular cliffs, quaint villages, unspoiled landscape and the oldest prehistoric temples in the world? When I wander leisurely around this unique area of divine creation, inhaling the beauty of it all, I always feel blessed to be alive and well and able to really appreciate and enjoy this heaven on earth.

Resorts

Sliema

The picturesque town of Sliema sits on a peninsula enjoying two waterfronts, one flanking the Mediterranean, and the other looking across Marsamxett Harbour into the eyes of Valletta. This is now the most fashionable resort in Malta offering up-market shopping, fine dining, classy hotels and apartments, and an important status symbol for those lucky enough to have acquired an address here.

Sliema got its name from a chapel dedicated to The Our Lady of The Sea and Sliem is the Maltese word meaning peace or serenity. It is quite a large residential town with a population of around 15,000 locals, housing also a significant number of expatriates that reside there temporarily.

Sliema was once a quiet fishing village and a little summer resort that attracted the wealthier Valletta residents. Elegant houses and villas were built and soon it grew into an important residential area and a hub for shopping, cafes and restaurants. In recent years the tourism potential of the area was developed and promoted with great success and now Sliema is the first tourist resort in Malta with the town expanding rapidly with a myriad of shops, hotels and apartment blocks.

Sliema is surrounded by the rich blue Mediterranean and the promontory offers spectacular views across to Valletta, an area that is now a hive of commercial activity. This is where all the harbour cruise operators have their little jetties, and every day, all along the Strand Road, the persistent salespeople work the crowds, frantically courting business, and through their tenacity and sales skills, manages to fill the many cruisers with tourists of every nationality, taking them to every nook and cranny of the Grand Harbour, returning them safe, highly impressed and delighted.

Apart from the harbour activity, Sliema is all about shopping. Up to a couple of years ago, the main shopping area was in the centre of the town between the two waterfronts, where many big international stores boomed, and were complimented by local independent shops, restaurants and boutiques. It was, and is still, a buzzing area of the town, but now, the development of Tigne Point has transformed shopping, not only for Sliema, but for the whole of Malta. This is located at one end of the town on an area jutting out into the harbour, and it is just massive.

87

It comprises hotels, apartments, infrastructure, and a three-tier shopping mall, all designed and finished to world-class standards. The mall, in particular, is spectacular with at least one hundred of the world's top brand names located here. I must say that I'm hugely impressed with these wonderful new facilities, and as I return each year I'm pleased to see it flourishing and successful, because this was a most courageous leap forward by the developers, and the government that backed this important project.

A small bridge situated at the end of Sliema Strand Road on the Gzira waterfront, leads to Manoel Island, a historic islet and an important landmark covering an area of some 30 hectares in the harbour between Sliema and Valletta. The Island's main feature is Fort Manoel, an 18th century fortification constructed by the Knights of St John. The fort was named in honour of the Grand Master and with its garrison of 500 men it was deemed virtually impregnable at the time.

After suffering devastating attacks and a series of direct hits during air raids in the Second World War, Fort Manoel was reduced to a shadow of its former magnificence. Sadly, the situation was worsened by the decades of neglect and vandalism that overtook the place after the British forces moved out of Malta. Several years and millions of Euro later, this historic gem has now been almost fully restored and further ambitious plans are in train for the historic little leaf-shaped island.

The other very well-known historic structure on Manoel Island is the Lazaretto. Built from 1643, the Lazaretto was first used as a quarantine centre and, later, as a hospital and Military base. Today the Lazaretto is in a critical state of repair but will be fully restored and re-used as part of the proposed new heritage regeneration process.

Manoel Island is an established yachting centre and includes an extensive yacht repair facility considered to be one of the best in the Mediterranean. A fully fledged 350-berth yacht marina also features in the plans for Manoel Island's further redevelopment which also envisages the provision of leisure facilities, gardens, walkways, museums and other cultural attractions.

Located beside the bridge that links Sliema with Manoel Island, there's one other little hidden treasure I want to mention. I discovered 'The Ducks Village' a few years ago, and today it looks as quaint and charming as the first day I spotted it. A little rocky enclosure, fenced off from the road with netting wire fencing, but with open access to the harbour waters, its population consists of hundreds of various fowl species: ducks, drakes, hens of all shapes and colours, guinea fowl, pigeons, and even multicoloured rabbits. They all live happily together in a little inclusive community, scratching around or swimming by day, and sleeping in little ornate coops by night. It is financed by voluntary donations, plus help from the local council, and since its creation about twenty years ago, it has delighted children of all ages, and thousands of tourists too, that were just lucky to find it.

Over the past few decades, Sliema's popularity has been steadily gaining momentum and it is now becoming a highly sought after area by both locals and tourists. With an abundance of top class amenities, spectacular sea views and a lively modern ambience, you'll find that Sliema is buzzing with exuberance and positive activity. I always find this little town delightful and exhilarating, and with its numerous bars, beach lidos, fine dining, delightful and colourful ice cream parlours, cafes, and stylish shopping malls, I'm spoiled for choice and for me there's never a dull moment in Sliema.

St Julian's

St. Julian's is almost unrecognisable from the little sheltered fishing village it once was; it is now one of Malta's busiest and most popular resorts. Most of it is new or upgraded, but one little spot, the real heart of the village that wraps around St Julian's Bay, hasn't changed for centuries. Here the picture-postcard scene is just captivating, with its relaxing atmosphere and old world charm. It is a quaint, cosy little harbour, an eyeful of idyllic beauty. The little bay is awash with colour and activity. Anchored and weaving gently, are a little flotilla of traditional 'Luzzu' fishing boats, that always seem to be painted a more vivid red, blue and yellow here, than anywhere else around the island. Tucked away in the far corner, under the road level is a little ancient boat repair workshop, still busy serving the fishermen, as it has done for many decades. Around the perimeter, at water level, are a myriad of restaurants and cafes booming with business, serving hundreds of diners sitting around open-air tables. Of course, much of the development of St. Julian's is modern, trendy and upmarket. The new resort-style development is Portomaso, an exclusive complex on the east coast of Spinola Bay. Dominating everything there is the giant 'Portamaso Tower,' a massive blue and terracotta office block, Malta's only skyscraper, and a landmark that is visible over a wide area. The world famous Hilton Hotel, with its extensive Conference Centre attached, occupies a prime location, and alongside is the state of the art marina, full of luxury yachts, indicating the attraction this area has for the wealthy elite. No less exclusive, is the complex of fashionable apartments, chic, stylish and expensive, no doubt, owned and occupied by millionaires, because this is a development designed to attract the mega-rich, and I get the feeling that the promoters have succeeded spectacularly.

PACEVILLE

Just a short walk up town to a maze of narrow streets full of cafes, bars and disco clubs is the area known as Paceville, the nightlife capital of Malta. This is the village that never sleeps, where the youth from all over the island congregate every night, especially at weekends, dine, wine and dance to loud music 'till the small hours, sometimes antagonising the settled community with their exuberant partying, and occasionally attracting the attention of the police, who strive valiantly to maintain peace and order which they generally succeed in doing.

A little further north is the picturesque St Georges Bay. In contrast to the high octane and boisterous mood of Paceville, this is a quiet, peaceful and cosy village surrounding a delightful little sandy beach and flanked by several upmarket hotel developments. This little gem is tucked away in a corner of St Julian's and it took me quite a few years to discover it. I now pay a visit every year, spending a few hours basking in the sunshine, always leaving happy and refreshed.

DRAGONARA PALACE

At the tip of the headland, Dragonara Point is the location of Malta's premier casino, gaming and entertainment centre. The casino is housed in a magnificent 19th-century seaboard summer mansion, Dragonara Palace, built by the Marquis Scicluna, with a surrounding colonnaded veranda that abuts directly onto the sea. It retains many of the original architectural and interior design features, which have been successfully adapted to the requirements of casino patrons, a combination of luxury, glamour and excitement, with an extensive bar and a highly rated restaurant. The Dragonara Palace was first converted for use as a casino in 1964 and is part of the huge Dragonara Resort of which the prestigious Westin Dragonara Resort Hotel is the main feature.

St Julian's is a town of contrasting characteristics. From the exquisite old world charm of St Julian's bay, to the grandeur of Portomaso, to the peaceful waters of St Georges Bay, it is certainly well endowed with interesting features for tourists to explore. In recent years it has become a bustling centre of activity with crowded streets and traffic gridlock. This is an indication of its growing popularity as one of Malta's top resorts and if ways can be found to ease the congestion the future will be bright and visitor numbers will continue to grow.

BALLUTA BAY

While I have great affection for the resorts of Sliema and St Julian's, it is the sea-side promenade extending from one to the other that I really admire and appreciate. This is the Tower Road which has been developed into a charming tree-lined walkway and is a joy for walkers, joggers and strollers like me who just like to meander along and enjoy the wonderful views of the blue Mediterranean.

Halfway between the two resorts is the pleasant little Balluta Bay nestled in a quiet corner, shaded by trees and with quaint little cafe bars and lots of seating. Here, along by the waterside a pathway is provided which give walkers the cool freshness of the sea and the pleasure of lingering a while in the beautiful gardens watching the children play, the wild cats roam and the sun smiling down. Above on the main street is the imposing Carmelite Church with the Carmelite Convent beside it. This is an impressive landmark, visible widely, with its exterior a rare example of Gothic Revival.

For me the striking feature of this little bay is the iconic Balluta Buildings. This is an apartment-block built in the 1920s and is regarded as Malta's finest example of Art Nouveau. With a wonderful facade featuring two huge arches, intricate motifs of angels and terraced profile, those buildings are simply ornate and beautiful.

The Tower Road promenade continues all the way from St Julian's to Tigne Point in Sliema. This is the most popular prom-walk in Malta. They come from all over the island, especially in summer, to stroll along, to savour the special feeling of wellbeing, and to enjoy the delights of this unique promenade. When I'm in Malta I never miss an opportunity to join them and enjoy this rare pleasure too.

Qawra

Qawra lies between Buġibba and Salina in the north, and is a popular tourists resort with many hotels and restaurants. Although there are no sandy beaches, many people swim off the rocks, which provide ample space for sun bathing. It is a popular area with tourists who like to enjoy a peaceful and relaxing holiday in an idyllic location. The seaside resort is just 17.6 kilometres (10.9 miles) away from Valletta, the capital city of Malta. It is an ideal centre for exploring the island of Malta, with an excellent road network, many car-hire facilities, and the bus terminus located in the town centre.

Around 1638, the Knights of St. John built Qawra Tower at Qawra Point. A battery was built around it in 1715, while an entrenchment wall was added in the 1760s. This is one of the many watch towers built by the Knights and this one watches St. Paul's Bay to the west and Salina Bay to the east. The tower is now a restaurant, and parts of the entrenchment wall can still be seen.

The resort of Qawra was built with the general idea of attracting British tourists, and its hotels, holiday apartments, restaurants, cafes, shops, bars, casinos, and other tourist facilities have a distinct British ambience. Hotels offer long-stay winter holidays, ideal for retired UK sun seekers, and British football is shown live in almost all pubs and clubs.

Water sports dominate the shoreline, and although there are no sandy beaches, swimming, sunbathing and diving are still very popular activities. There is a long promenade that stretches for around 3km all the way to St. Paul's Bay. This walkway outlines the rocky shoreline, and provides fantastic views of the open sea. It offers a perfect space for leisurely walks and jogs, especially during the evenings, when the sea and sun merge in spectacular colours.

THE NATIONAL AQUARIUM

Malta's National Aquarium only recently opened its doors to the public and already it is proving a huge attraction for the Maltese and for tourists from all over the world. Opened in 2013, this glass and metal star-fish-shaped building is set in a sublime position on the Qawra headland, with endless views of the Mediterranean Sea.

The aquarium features 26 tanks and over 175 different species of fish. Spread over 20,000 square meters the complex includes a public garden, ample parking, facilities for local dive schools and catering facilities, including a bespoke beach club with an inviting infinity pool appropriately named 'Cafe Del Mar' as well as tourist services and souvenirs shops. The complex also includes a fabulous children's playground (free of charge) and stunning views from its Le Nave restaurant and outdoor cafe.

The main tank in the aquarium is the home for various species from the Indian Ocean including two varieties of shark species. Approximately 12 meters in diameter the main tank also includes a water tunnel allowing visitors to walk through and feel a real sense of immersion in this underwater world. Amongst others, there is also a selection of Mediterranean fish, commonly found in Maltese waters and replicas of historical artefacts that surround the Maltese sea floor. Additional features at the complex include an exhibition space, touch pools, veterinary and quarantine facilities and a class room facility. The public garden will also provide various other recreational activities.

Having watched the construction of this beautiful complex I am hugely impressed with the finished project. I know that it was funded mainly by the EU and would not have been possible without the European cash, but I still applaud the Malta Government and the Tourist Board for their vision and foresight in the creation of this beautiful world class project.

MALTA CLASSIC CAR MUSEUM

One of the more unusual treats in the Resort of Qawra is the Malta Classic Car Museum located in Tourist Street just a few paces from the Bus Terminus. It is the first and only automobile museum in Malta and it is a big attraction for visitors to the area.

The museum is home to a vast collection of cars and motorcycles, juke boxes, scale model collections and plenty of memorabilia, which are always increasing; the latest venture being a collection of ladies clothes from the 40s to the 60s. Here the guests have an opportunity to go back in time by viewing this varied and interesting exhibition and watch a film in a state of the art cinema that seats sixty-five and has continuous running documentaries. Patrons are allowed to take photographs of all the exhibits and afterwards visit the cafeteria that is open for refreshments.

The idea of a museum was conceived and created by Carol Galea, a Maltese motoring enthusiast and for him, this Malta Classic Car Museum is the fulfilment of a life-long dream. The lovely 3000 square metre museum, reached through a regal marble staircase, today comprises classics such as Alfa Romeo, Austin, Jaguar, Fiat, Ford, MG, Mini, Sunbeam, Triumph, as well as the most modern BMWs, Jaguar and Ferrari. There are also classic motorbikes such as the BSA, Vespa and Lambretta. Every car on display can be reached from all angles, making the enthusiast feel much more at ease to inspect thoroughly without being forbidden to take photographs.

Apart from the over one hundred items on display, there is also a great variety of jukeboxes, slot machines, life size models, memorabilia and posters. Carol himself is responsible for the remarkable photographic collection capturing a past motoring epoch. The Malta Classic Car Museum is a marvellous vehicle exhibition of international standard that is unlike anything else on the island, and for those lovers of old classic vintage cars a visit here will be a nostalgic and enjoyable trip down memory lane.

SALINA BAY SALT PANS

Salt is known to have been harvested and collected on the Maltese Islands for over 2,000 years. The production of salt is a highly traditional affair that has been passed down from generation to generation.

The Knights of Saint John constructed the Salina Bay salt pans during the 16th century, when salt was an absolute necessity for preserving food. By the 1620's, Salina Bay was producing so much salt that large amounts could be exported.

Salt production on the islands reached the peak around 1870 with around 75% of the salt produced being exported. Unfortunately a series of harsh storms in 1979, 1990 and 2003 badly damaged the Salina Bay salt-pans and salt production in Malta declined drastically.

Recently a big renovation project has been completed making them serviceable and productive again. The project, 75 per cent of which is funded by the EU, includes the restoration and cleaning of 35 salt pans, which have returned to production.

A visitors centre is also being built detailing the Maltese Islands history and production of this most valuable of minerals. The Salina Bay salt pans have been described as a national treasure and they are now a significant tourist attraction in this important holiday zone of Qawra, Bugibba and St Paul's Bay.

Bugibba

Buġibba is a zone within St. Paul's Bay in the Northern Region of Malta. It is situated adjacent to Qawra, and it is a popular tourist resort, containing numerous hotels, restaurants, pubs, clubs, a cinema, and a casino. This area has only been a tourist resort for the last 30 years or so but progress has been fast and the area has developed rapidly since that time and is now a significant holiday resort. Bugibba is also a large residential area for both Maltese and permanent residents from the UK and other countries.

Its coastline is rocky but has many small inlets offering access to the clear, shallow water of the Mediterranean which are all well utilised in the summer months by the local people. Additionally, a 'man-made' beach has been constructed in Bugibba close to the Dolmen Hotel although access to the sea is still over a rocky shoreline. The beach is open between April and October every year.

The recently constructed Water Park is a new attraction in Bugibba. It is ideal for children as it includes a number of exciting features, such as water loops, water umbrellas, parasols, a bucket tower, a palm spring and two water cannons. The park is built on 800 square metres of land and can accommodate up to 50 children providing lots of refreshing fun and exciting pleasure.

Bugibba's biggest attraction is Bay Square, located in the heart of the town facing the seafront with fantastic views of the blue ocean all the way across to St Paul's Island. The square serves as a hub for the shops, bars and restaurants, and is a delightful spot to linger and enjoy the surroundings from the many comfortable benches arranged in its centre. The square comes alive especially at night during the warmer months as the main nightlife in the area is located here. Regular music concerts are held in the square and together with the live music in the pubs; there is no shortage of music and entertainment.

St Paul's Bay

Saint Paul's Bay is a town in the Northern Region of Malta and with its neighbours Buġibba and Qawra, form Malta's largest, seaside resort. The resident population is around 20.000 persons but this goes up to about 60,000 during the period of June to September. The increase is due both to Maltese summer residents and tourists in hotels and apartments in Buġibba, Qawra and St Paul's Bay.

St Paul's Bay is densely populated with locals and permanently resident foreign nationals. Although its coastline is virtually all rocky, it does have many small inlets with easy access to the clear, shallow water of the bays which are all extremely well used in the summer months by the local residents. St Paul's Bay, although very close to both Bugibba and Qawra, would be considered a much quieter location by comparison with these neighbours.

For visitors like me who prefer a relaxing and peaceful vacation, St Paul's Bay is just perfect. I have lived here and I have nothing but fond memories of this idyllic spot. It began as a little fishing village and despite its extensive growth, it still is and feels a little fishing village. Deep in the heart of the bay the residents are all Maltese. They are proud of their tradition and their unique heritage. This is the sacred spot where St Paul scrambled ashore after being shipwrecked on his way to his trial in Rome in 60 AD. While here he gave them Christianity, which they have cherished ever since and Paul is revered as their Patron Saint.

WIGNACOURT TOWER

Wignacourt Tower is a bastioned watchtower located in St. Paul's Bay. It was the first of six Wignacourt towers to be built, was completed in 1610, and is now the oldest surviving watchtower in Malta.

By the end of the 16th century, Malta's harbour area was extensively fortified. However, the rest of the islands were virtually undefended, and the coastline was open to attacks by Ottomans or Barbary corsairs. Alof de Wignacourt, set out to build a series of towers around the coastline, which were personally funded by him and came to be known as the Wignacourt Towers.

The first tower was built to protect St. Paul's Bay, and was called Wignacourt Tower after the Grand Master. On 7 November 1609, plans and a model of the tower were presented to the Order's council. The first stone was blessed and laid on 10 February 1610, and the accompanying ceremony was personally attended by Wignacourt himself. A coastal battery was added to the tower in 1715 to house two 18-pounder guns. Buttressing was added to the lower half of the structure in around 1761.

The tower's original entrance was on the first floor, and it was approached by a drawbridge from a flight of stone steps. The steps were removed in the 1950s when the road in front of the tower was widened. An entrance was added on the ground floor. Wignacourt Tower was restored between 1973 and 1976. During restoration, the tower's turrets were completely rebuilt. Since 1998, the tower has been a museum, and its exhibits include models of various fortifications found in the Maltese islands, reproductions of items used by the tower's occupants in the 17th and 18th centuries, old photos and a restored cannon.

In 2010, the 400th anniversary of the tower was celebrated by the St. Paul's Bay Local Council, the Festa Committee and Din l-Art Ħelwa by a series of events including re-enactments, tours, discussions and traditional Maltese folklore.

The tower was restored and cleaned once again in 2015 and perched on a high point overlooking the picturesque bay, it is an impressive landmark. It is open to the public and many tourists find a visit informative and enjoyable.

ST PAUL'S BAY CHURCHES

St. Paul's Bay has always been a summer resort, and with the increase of summer residents at the beginning of the present century, St. Paul's Sanctuary became too small. The Countess Anna Bugeja, in remembrance of the 1900

Holy Year, built a church dedicated to the Sorrows of Our Lady and gave it to the Franciscan Conventuals. The church became a parish in 1905 and was considerably enlarged in 1960-1979. The parish population is now 5000 consisting of 2100 families.

This is a beautiful church with an impressive facade and an even more attractive interior. The layout, decor, paintings and embellishments are just stunning. While staying in St Paul's Bay some years ago I was a frequent visitor to this ornate treasure and I always left impressed and inspired.

ST PAUL'S SHIPWRECK CHURCH

In the square by the waterfront is the tiny St Paul's Shipwreck Church. It was built on the spot where St Paul is believed to have come ashore after being shipwrecked on his way to his trial in Rome and his subsequent execution. The first church was built here in the fourteenth century and the site has been a shrine of worship ever since. During the World War 11 bombing raids, the church was destroyed, and today's church is a new reconstruction. The story of Paul's shipwreck and his stay in Malta is detailed in the Bible and the relevant chapter is shown in various languages on plaques outside the church.

This is a miniature church of stone structure with a plain interior. In contrast to other Malta churches it is not richly embellished, but it does have an impressive painting depicting St Paul's shipwreck. For the residents of St Paul's Bay, this little sanctuary is a spiritual treasure that they revere and cherish. During Masses and services they fill the little church and every evening for the 5.30 Mass, it is full of devout parishioners.

ST PAUL'S ISLAND

Directly across the bay is a little island rock known for centuries as St Paul's Island. This is believed to be the area where the shipwreck occurred as Paul was being taken to Rome to be tried as a political rebel. The ship with 274 others on board was caught in a violent storm and broke up in the region of this little island. By some miracle which Paul had foreseen, all on board, though non-swimmers, managed to reach the shore which they then discovered was Malta.

The welcome given to the survivors is described in the Acts of the Apostles (XXVIII) by St. Luke:

"And later we learned that the island was called Malta. And the people who lived there showed us great kindness, and they made a fire and called us all to warm ourselves... "

As the fire was lit, Paul was bitten by a poisonous snake but he suffered no ill effects. The islanders took this as a sign that he was a special man. This scene is depicted in many religious works of art on the Islands.

In 1844 a prominent statue of Saint Paul was erected on the island. It was sculpted by Segismondo Dimech from Valletta and Salvatore Dimech from Lija. The statue was officially inaugurated and blessed on 21 September 1845. It has since been restored a number of times, first in 1996, then in 2007, in 2014, and 2015.

Until the 1930s, a farmer called Vincenzo Borg, lived on the island. His farmhouse was located close to the statue of Saint Paul. He abandoned the dwelling and the fields on the island just before World War II started. Since it was abandoned, the upper rooms have collapsed and the structure is now in ruins.

Pope John Paul II visited the island by boat during his visit to Malta in 1990. Many tourists including myself visit the little island as part of a day cruise which also takes in Comino and Gozo. It is a reassuring sight for the Maltese to gaze across and see their patron saint perched high on the rock, his hands outstretched and watching over them, keeping them faithful to the Christianity that he gave them almost 2000 years ago.

Mellieha

Mellieha could be described as a small town or a large village. It has a population of about 10,000 and is perched on a group of hills on the northwest coast of Malta. It overlooks Mellieħa Bay, which includes Għadira Bay, the largest sandy beach in Malta. To the east of the town and bay, there is the Selmun peninsula, and St Paul's Island lies about 80 metres off the coast. Mistra Bay lies close to Selmun, and this marks the boundary between Mellieħa and St Paul's Bay.

Mellieħa was once an isolated 15th century hamlet and was abandoned for a couple of centuries because of its vulnerability to pirate and Saracen attack. Inhabited again in the early 18th century, it has since developed into a flourishing town though it still retains a quaint historic centre with narrow hilly streets and stepped alleys.

It is now a popular tourist destination during the summer months, well known for its sandy beaches, with the most popular being Għadira Bay and Golden Bay. Nearby Ċirkewwa is a well-known dive site, some of its attractions being the wrecks of MV *Rozi* and the P29 patrol boat. Tourism continues to be aggressively promoted and developed and in 2009, Mellieħa was awarded the title of European Destination of Excellence due to its sustainable initiatives.

But despite this rapid tourism development, Mellieha is still full of authentic character and old world charm. In recent years its idyllic location has attracted lots of Maltese who have built elegant houses and villas there, and together with a perfusion of apartments and hotels dotting the hills and slopes, the result is a picturesque and vibrant resort. For me, it's nice to see that it still manages to preserve its quaint character with its narrow streets, steep stepped alleys, old shops and charming hospitable residents.

My favourite part of Mellieha is the north end which is the town's real historic area. This is where the magnificent Mellieha Parish Church stands on the edge of Mellieha Ridge. Built in 1881 and dedicated to the Birth of Our Lady, it is a magnificent church, dominating the Mellieha skyline and from around the church there are spectacular views over the lower green and fertile country side and Mellieha bay. It is also where an attractive cluster of medieval chapels are hewn into the rock and also where the people sheltered during World War 11, and those underground shelters can be seen today.

SANCTUARY AND CHURCH OF OUR LADY

Almost directly beneath the parish church is the Sanctuary and Church of Our Lady which is now a national shrine. This is an amazing structure set in a cave burrowed in to the rock face consisting of a crypt, a sacristy and a little church that is stunningly beautiful. The dimly lit interior of the church is charming in its simplicity, its walls are marble, the ceiling is low, and the altar has two marble columns supporting an arch of gold montage.

A fresco behind the altar of the Madonna with Jesus in her arms is believed to have been painted by St Luke in 60 AD when he was on the island with St Paul after the shipwreck. The centuries have taken their toll on the painting but it is still there to be admired and cherished by the devout congregations who attend Mass and the other services in this unique little Sanctuary.

GROTTO OF OUR LADY

A short distance from the two churches is located the Grotto of Our Lady. It is hidden away underground and can be reached by a long descending stairway. When you get to the bottom you find a little cave chapel and a shrine dedicated to Our Lady. It is believed that an Italian merchant paid for the grotto to be dug into the rock in the 12th century.

Inside the grotto is a statue of the Blessed Virgin in an enclosure that has a stream from an unknown source flowing through it. This water is said to have remarkable healing powers and down the years people with ailments and illnesses have prayed here, were cured, and came back to give thanks, leaving a memento to add to the existing collection adorning the walls.

I always pay a visit to this little shrine when I'm in Mellieha. It is so deep underground, so simple and peaceful, dimly lit with only the little candles left by visitors flickering in the silence, that you get a strange feeling of peaceful solitude. It's as if the big world above doesn't matter anymore and you have found a new little haven of peace and tranquillity. But reality soon sets in when you start climbing those numerous steep steps that leave you breathless and take you back into the real world.

MELLIEHA BAY

The largest and best beach in the Maltese Islands is located in Mellieha Bay which is about 2km from the town of Mellieha. It is a beautiful sandy beach about 1km long and is very safe for families and swimmers because the clear water is still only ankle deep one hundred metres into the sea. It is also patrolled by lifeguards and being adjacent to the main road; there is ample space for parking.

The problem with this lovely beach is that it is now too popular with the Maltese and tourists. In summer it becomes very crowded. Day-trippers, swimmers, surfers and lovers of all forms of water sports make this idyllic spot a hive of activity and a centre of wonderful pleasure and recreation.

MELLIEHA AIR RAID SHELTERS

Deep in the heart of Mellieha is a maze of rock-cut shelters where the people took refuge during World War 11 to escape Hitler's cruel aerial bombardment. I have visited them and I was surprised and astonished. I found it amazing to see how a people under siege, with their lives and their children's lives in peril used their ingenuity to defend themselves against deadly attacks of terror and firepower, and in doing so, endured the most appalling hardship to survive.

Down in those cramped shelters I saw living quarters that were hewn from the rock with bare hands and primitive tools. I saw little hospital wards where babies were born and the sick attended to, and I saw a system of regulation and order that was applied to preserve privacy and dignity, vital in such crowded underground living.

Those Air Raid Shelters are retained exactly as they were seventy-five years ago and they provide a fascinating image of a turbulent time in Malta's past, a test of a people's courage and resilience that was confronted and endured with bravery and dignity. The shelters are open to the public and are well worth a visit to see how Maltese families coped with adversity and survived Hitler's onslaught of terror.

MARSAXLOKK

When one sees the name Marsaxlokk written down it looks a difficult word to pronounce, but after a few attempts I eventually cracked it. It is pronounced 'Marsa-shlock' and derives from *marsa* (the port) and *xlokk* (the sirocco wind). It is the biggest and most picturesque fishing village in Malta and as a must-visit for tourists, it is always a highlight of their visit to the Maltese Islands.

Set on an inlet on the northern side of Marsaxlokk Bay in Malta's south east corner, this quaint village is a treasure trove of traditional character, colourful ambience and old world charm. The bay is alive with all shapes and sizes of fishing boats and the promenade is swarming with fishermen, some unloading fish, some buying them, some working on boats and some sitting on fish boxes mending their nets. It is a joy to linger a while and just gaze.

But the promenade is so long and spacious that it is also a busy market place selling a myriad of quality souvenirs and the famous hand-made Maltese lace. The 'Flea Market,' as it is called is open on a small scale every day but on Sundays it is a major event involving a multitude of traders and attracting bargain-hunters from all over Malta as well as hordes of tourists who come to savour the atmosphere.

But for most tourists the best part of the long promenade is the open air restaurants where they can relax and enjoy the amazing fresh fish dishes expertly cooked and presented. This is a truly unique dining experience. All around is the true fish culture, the fishy smell is everywhere and the tables are adorned with the most succulent fish cuisine. It's a perfect combination and it's no surprise to see the ever increasing influx of tourists availing of this heavenly ambience.

Most of Malta's fish supplies are caught by the fishermen of Marsaxlokk. Swordfish, tuna, and the popular 'lampuki' are the big catch between spring and late autumn. On weekdays, most of the fish are taken to the fish-market in Valletta, but on Sundays the catch is retailed by fishermen in the open on the quay.

Malta with its extensive fishing industry has been relatively lucky in avoiding sea tragedies down through the decades. In 1924 a storm cost the lives of fishermen but for the following eighty-four years, not one boat or life was lost. Sadly, that all changed in July 2008 when a fishing tragedy occurred that rocked the nation, causing unspeakable anguish for the crew and their families.

It was a family owned boat from Marsaxlokk, named 'Simshar' and while fishing off the coast of Sicily an explosion and fire destroyed the boat leaving the crew clinging on to a flimsy makeshift raft in the middle of the Mediterranean. The crew were the skipper, his elderly father, his 11-year-old son, and two young crewmen. While a massive search involving naval vessels, aircraft and the whole fishing fleet continued for eight days without a sighting, the crew were dying one by one until eventually the little raft was found. The skipper was the only one still clinging on but was just a few hours from death. He was rescued and was the only survivor who lived to tell the horrible tale.

The tragic story is now recaptured in print and on screen. The book 'The Crying Sea' written by Paddy Cummins (Yours Truly) gives a harrowing account of the tragedy from beginning to end and the story is now a major international film 'Simshar.'

I have spent many sombre days in Marsaxlokk chatting to the fishing community while researching the book. They have put all that behind them and now when I go there I find again the old vibrant and friendly atmosphere that always characterised this delightful fishing village. I never tire of going there and I think most visitors would say the same.

MARSASCALA

Marsascala is a sea-side village in the South Eastern Region of Malta that has grown around the small harbour at the head of Marsaskala Bay, a long narrow inlet also known as Marsaskala Creek. The population in winter is about 12,000 people, but this swells to over 20,000 in summer as many Maltese families have summer homes there and it is fast becoming an attractive holiday resort. A prominent landmark is the beautiful parish church which is dedicated to St. Anne, whose feast is celebrated at the end of July and is a big occasion in Marsascala.

Marsascala has always been, and still is a fishing village. The picturesque bay is full of colourful fishing boats and pleasure boats of all shapes and sizes. The village has expanded rapidly in recent years and now reaches to both sides of the bay. The attractive promenade continues all the way to St Thomas Bay with views of low shelving rocks, beautiful scenery and saltpans. During the summer months Marsascala is buzzing with life and leisure activity. Its many hotels and apartments are always fully booked and for those thousands who holiday in Marsascala it is the place to be, enjoying the friendly hospitality and the hot sunshine.

Despite its rapid growth in recent years, Marsascala is largely unspoiled. It still has the feel of a traditional fishing village. But it has also moved with the modern times, embracing the culture of tourism and providing first class services for its visitors. Here you will find some of the best restaurants, many of them specializing in typical Maltese fish cuisine. Marsascala is still one of the undiscovered gems of the Maltese Islands. It is less populated than the larger more upmarket resort areas. Anyone looking for a more peaceful area to enjoy the sea front, beautiful views, fish cuisine and scuba diving will find Marsascala to be a great holiday resort.

Towns

MOSTA

Shrouded by myths, Mosta is considered to be one of Malta's most historical places of interest and is now a very important tourist location. A large town in central Malta, with a population of about 20,000 people, Mosta is always buzzing with hordes of tourists mingling with local residents and the commercial sector busy and flourishing. Being located in the centre of Malta and with a road connection between south and north, the main street has to carry a huge volume of traffic, mainly buses and coaches, on their way from Valletta to Buġibba, St. Paul's Bay, Qawra, Xemxija, Ċirkewwa and Mellieħa.

Mosta is connected with several local popular legends. The town is surrounded by many historical places of interest, including the Victoria Lines, which were built by the British Empire as a defence mechanism against land invasion from the North. But by far the greatest treasure in Mosta is an iconic building dominating the town centre and attracting visitors from all corners of the world.

The 'Mosta Dome' is a gigantic church with the third largest unsupported dome in the world. Built between 1833 and 1860 on the site of a previous church, the plan was based on the Pantheon in Rome. It was designed by George Grognet de Vasse, a French citizen resident in Mosta. Local residents, at that time totalling not more than 1500, built the church with their own hands and their own cash collections. It took them 27 years to complete but the result is a tourist attraction of world standard. Grognet was a perfectionist and he chose the type of stone by getting one slab from each quarry operating in the Islands. He then proceeded to test their durability. In the end he chose the stone from a quarry in Mosta.

The people of Mosta dismiss accusations of deliberate pomposity in building such a huge dome on their church. It had to be those proportions because the church was constructed around the existing church which could not be demolished until the new one was complete. In fact the old church came in handy as scaffolding while building the new one. The facade of the 'Retunda' is immensely impressive and being so high and of such huge proportions, it can be seen almost all over the island of Malta.

The interior is just spellbinding with its size, design and decor. A coffered ceiling of gilded stone-carved flowers set on a blue background and a floor on inlaid marble gives a feeling of rich splendour. There are eight splendid side altars and a magnificent high altar. The murals behind the side altars, painted by the famous Maltese artist, Giuseppe Cali, are simply beautiful. The whole interior, lavishly decorated by local artists and trimmed with gold leaf is a joy to behold.

The Mosta Retunda, as it is best known, is dedicated to The Assumption of Our Lady and a very popular feast among the locals as well as the tourists is the feast of the Assumption of Our Blessed Lady on the 15th August. This day is a public holiday and is celebrated with lots of music, food and fireworks. The church had an amazing escape in 1942 when it could have been demolished by a direct hit from a German bomber but by some miracle it was granted a reprieve.

The location of Mosta near to Ta' Qali airfield placed it right in the path of attacking planes during World War 11. On one such raid on the 9th April 1942, several bombs were dropped around the church, with one actually piercing the dome, landing on the floor where three hundred people were attending Mass, and incredibly, it failed to explode. No one was injured, the dome was only slightly damaged, and to commemorate the miracle, the empty shell of the bomb can be seen today in the sacristy of the church.

Another renowned attraction in Mosta is the Speranza Chapel which is situated close to the Speranza Valley. Legend has it that during the Turkish invasion between 1760 and 1761, a young girl and her siblings were taking care of the family's sheep. The siblings managed to escape but the little girl could not run fast enough so she found refuge in a cave where she prayed to Our Lady who intervened and created a spider web over the opening of the cave. The Turkish invaders did not look for her in the cave as the web was still intact.

The town of Mosta is surrounded by many historical places of interest, including the famous and historic Victoria Lines. Those were originally known as the North West Front and sometimes unofficially known as the *Great Wall of Malta*. They are a line of fortifications flanked by defensive towers that spans 12 kilometres along the width of Malta, dividing the north of the island from the more heavily populated south.

The Victoria Lines run along a natural geographical barrier known as the Great Fault, from Madliena in the east, through the limits of the town of Mosta in the centre of the island, to Binġemma and the limits of Rabat, on the west coast. The complex network of linear fortifications known collectively as the Victoria Lines, cuts across the width of the island north of the old capital of Mdina, and built by the British Empire as a defence against land invasion, is a unique monument of military architecture and can still be viewed today.

Another item of interest to those visiting Mosta would be the historical farmhouse overlooking the valley of Wied il-ghasel. This old farmstead was the property of the noble family of the Marquis Mallia Tabone. It is now run by the Philanthropic Society, 'Talent Mosti' in collaboration with the adjacent school council. It is now a busy resource hosting lots of exhibitions throughout the year.

The town of Mosta is now a bustling market town but is also a major tourist location. Traffic can be heavy especially in Constitution Street; the main artery that skirts around the 'Dome,' but it doesn't bother the thousands of visitors who flock to this amazing architectural and spiritual phenomenon. I'm sure they are all amazed by the eye-opener that is the Mosta Dome, and like me, depart uplifted and inspired.

Floriana

The town of Floriana is located just on the outskirts of the walled city of Valletta, It is part of the capital's landward fortifications which reach as far as the Portes des Bombes, the magnificent baroque arches which were the entrance gates on the main road approaching Valletta. The town dates back to 1634, and got its name when Grandmaster de Paule, sensing another attack by the Ottoman Turks, brought over an Italian engineer, Pietro Paolo Floriani, who built further massive fortifications and Floriana effectively became an entire fortress town in front of Valletta.

Sitting so close to the renowned capital city and sometimes seen as just a suburb of Valletta, the immense heritage and rich history of Floriana may not be fully appreciated but this area has many hidden treasures that are the equivalent of those in Valletta itself. The important buildings, monuments, churches and gardens, offer testimony to Malta's political and social history from the era of the Knights of St John to the present day. It has developed to be an important town in its own right, covering an area of 133 acres, with a population of around 2,600 people. The town offers an interesting mix of historic buildings, churches, gardens and monuments that shed a light on the Maltese history.

The Parish Church (1733-1792) is definitely the most dominant landmark in Floriana. It is dedicated to St Publius, the first Maltese Bishop of Malta who was martyred in Athens in 125 AD and is the patron saint of Floriana. According to tradition, when as leader of Malta he received St. Paul after he was shipwrecked and Paul converted him to Christianity. St. Publius is the first Maltese saint, and so the devotion of the Maltese towards him is great. Pope John Paul II visited this church during his stay in Malta in 1990.

This is a typically large Maltese parish church and stands majestically overlooking Granaries Square. But the church that impresses me most is Sarria Church. In the centre of Floriana, it is a small round church with a unique characteristic: it is the only church entirely designed by Mattia Preti, the iconic artist that adorned St John's Co-Cathedral. In 1676 a terrible plague ravaged the island. The Grand Master Nicolas Cotoner, in the hope of obtaining the help of the Holy Mary, asked Mattia Preti to hurriedly build a church dedicated to the Immaculate Conception. Preti designed a circular shaped chapel, similar to the Pantheon in Rome, and adorned the interior with an impressive circle of paintings depicting the Holy Mary and the Saints eradicating the plague. By Maltese standards this is a tiny church but its history, its design, and Preti's wonderful art work makes it a must-visit attraction for visitors to Floriana.

The Granaries are another intriguing feature of Floriana and are highly visible beside the main road as one travels in to Valletta. Situated in front of the parish church they consist of a huge square punctuated with a large number of stone slabs. The Granaries were built as an underground storage facility for grain by Grand Master Marino de Redin between 1657 and 1660. They simply look like a large open square, but underground, beneath the numerous stone caps are bell shaped grain storage silos, seventy six in total, capable of holding around sixty five tons each.

The silos remained in use until 1962, when a modern above-the-ground storage facility was built. Nowadays, the silos are empty but the square is used for concerts, festivals and mass political meetings.

I like to walk around Floriana and view all the interesting historical landmarks. The Wignacourt Water Tower, for example, commemorated the inauguration, in 1615, of the aqueduct system which brought water by gravity from the high grounds around Rabat to Floriana and Valletta. The Neo-Gothic Wesleyan Church, now Sir Robert Sammut Community Hall, and the Lion Fountain (1728), which served for a time as the only water supply for the inhabitants of Floriana.

Also of interest is the Mall; today a garden but once an area where the Knights played a kind of tennis. This narrow strip of greenery, clearly visible beside the road into Valletta, is dotted with statues and plaques commemorating events and personalities of Maltese 20th century history. Floriana is further beautified by the large number of gardens around the town. I like to visit the Sa Maison Gardens, the Argotti Gardens, and the Garden of Rest, all of which offer different views of Marsamxett Harbour. But of course the real treasure for me is the 'Waterfront', nestling beneath the bastions of Valletta and Floriana. This is where the millions of cruise visitors are welcomed and entertained in a magnificent and unique setting. But you don't have to step off a cruise liner to be enthralled and fascinated by the delights of the 'Waterfront'. I am always inspired and beguiled by the distinct character and old world charm of this seductive spot.

Floriana may be dwarfed in size and stature by the World Heritage City of Valletta, but it is a thriving modern town in its own right. It provides a massive multi-story car park, much appreciated by commuters to Valletta, the headquarters of the Maltese police force and the National Library are located here, and the renowned 5-Star Pheonicia Hotel stands proudly just outside the entrance gate to the capital city. This 1920s-style hotel has been a Malta icon since the 16th century and is a fine example of the island's revered architectural tradition. It has also been providing 5-Star luxury to the hordes of tourists who come from around the world and appreciate excellent service and genuine Maltese hospitality.

Marsa

Marsa is a town in the South Eastern Region of Malta, with a population of about 4,000 people. The name Marsa means 'the harbour.' It is located on the Marsa Creek, an inlet that includes the Grand Harbour on which the town is situated. A port was first established at Marsa by the Phoenicians and remains of Roman constructions have been found close to the town. It is thought that a foundry of the Order of the Knights of St. John may have been located there too.

Marsa has been mainly an industrialised zone. In recent years when the British developed the Portu Novu (the new port), industrial activity in the area grew rapidly and now it is quite a busy harbour town. The famous Malta

Shipyards are located here and plans for a large marina including a recreational area are also underway.

But I'm sure many visitors would be surprised to find two of Malta's most popular sporting attractions located in the heart of a highly industrialised town like Marsa. Well, I was a bit surprised too when I discovered them. But they are here: 'The Royal Malta Golf Club' and 'The Marsa Horse Race Track.

The Royal Malta Golf Club is positioned in beautifully maintained grounds and being centrally located in the Mediterranean it enjoys a wonderful climate providing excellent golfing conditions. The club was founded in 1888 when golf was played around the moats and bastions formed by the fortification walls of Valletta. One of the founding members was the then Duke of Edinburgh who was serving in Malta at the time and from whom the club received royal patronage. It moved to its present location in 1904, and is now situated in the grounds of the Marsa Sports Club and boasts of being one of only 63 Royal Golf Clubs.

There is only one racecourse in Malta, the Marsa Horse Race Track. Founded way back in in 1868, the Marsa course was said at that time to be one of the longest tracks in Europe. The first horse races were held there on the 12th and 13th of April 1869. The present racetrack was reconstructed in 1981 with new facilities and a grandstand for 2,000 spectators. Bars and shops were also added and now, as well as the local races, Marsa is sometimes used as a venue for international events such as the European Championship for Professional Drivers. These are all trotting races with the jockey riding a gig drawn by the horse. Occasionally, some traditional horse and jockey races are also run at the course.

When Her Majesty Queen Elizabeth II was visiting Malta for the Commonwealth Heads of Government Meeting in 2015, she was delighted to visit Maltese horse racing at Marsa race track. An avid rider herself, the Marsa complex reminded The Queen of her younger days when she used to ride horses during her stay in Malta. The day ended appropriately when the horse, 'ROYAL IN' was the winner of the Queen Elizabeth II Silver Race Final, a special race organised for the occasion. The winning trophy was awarded to the driver and owner by The Queen herself in the presence of Her Excellence the President of Malta, Marie Louise Coleiro Preca. A great day and a great boost for the race track.

Pembroke

Pembroke is a town in the Northern Region of Malta, and is considered to be the island's newest town. To the east is Paceville, the nightlife district of Malta, the coastal town and tourist hub of St. Julian's lies to the southeast, and the residential area of Swieqi lies to the south.

Pembroke covers an area of 2.3 km² and has a population of almost 4,000 people. The area hugs a coastal zone with a rocky beach, and the highest point lies at 64 meters (210 feet) above sea level. The whole area was formerly a British military base from the 1850s to 1979 and was named after Robert Henry Herbert, the 12th Earl of Pembroke and British Secretary at War in 1859. Pembroke was formerly part of St. Julian's and only officially became a town in 1993. It is now one of 68 localities in Malta, each having its own Local Council with its own Mayor and Deputy Mayor.

The first known buildings in the area of the town date back to the time of the Order of Saint John. The Knights built two Watch Towers on the extreme ends of the current Pembroke coast. The first of these is Saint George's Tower, which was built in 1638 as part of a series of coastal watch towers. The second tower, Madliena Tower, forms part of a network of 13 coastal watch towers, collectively known as the De Redin towers, which were built between 1658 and 1659 to protect the northern coast of Malta. These 13 towers adorn the official flag and emblem of Pembroke, reflecting the town's military heritage.

However, it was the British who were instrumental in the development and fortification of Pembroke by building a military base complete with a hospital, cemetery, school, parade grounds, training grounds and shooting ranges. The first barracks were constructed between 1859 and 1862 overlooking St. George's Bay and were named after England's patron saint, St. George. Later, other barracks were built and were named after the patron saints of Ireland and Scotland, St. Patrick and St. Andrew. Fort

Pembroke was built between 1875 and 1878 to safeguard the seaward approach towards the Grand Harbour.

Although the British army have long gone, the military heritage of Pembroke is still evident as several buildings from the British era survive to this day. The Pembroke Military Cemetery marks the repose of 593 casualties, including 315 from the Second World War. The cemetery also houses the Pembroke Memorial which commemorates 52 servicemen of the Second World War whose graves are in other parts of Malta. Their names appear on marble plaques in the plinth of the Cross of Sacrifice. The cemetery is open Monday to Friday.

During the Second World War and the ensuing blitz on Malta, Pembroke did not escape unscathed and has borne the scars from its share of the bombardment. In the later stages of the war, German prisoners of war were held in Pembroke's POW camp. By 1945 they reached 2500 prisoners and several of them were of Roman Catholic denomination. They built a small chapel which served the religious needs of the catholic troops and prisoners. The Chapel was formally blessed by the Archbishop of Malta Mikiel Gonzi in May 1946. During 1947, several prisoners were repatriated to Germany and on 9th February 1948, the last contingents of 787 Germans departed from Malta heading home to Germany. On 17th February 1948, No.1 (Malta) Prisoner of War Camp was officially disbanded.

Pembroke's background is military. This residential area started life as British barracks built in typical colonial style. When the British forces left Malta in the 1970s, the area was used for local housing and has since expanded with the building of modern, spacious houses and villas. Pembroke Battery, one of two from British times, still stands and is now being restored. The roads in Pembroke bear names such as Anzio, Alamein and Normandy - all reminiscent of British military activity in World War II. The barracks which remain have a certain charm as does the graceful Pembroke and Sandhurst Clock Towers.

Pembroke is now a young modern town and is becoming well known for hosting a high concentration of schools and educational institutions. For those interested in the history of the British military presence in Malta; Pembroke has it all.

Birkikara

Birkirkara is the largest, oldest and most densely inhabited town in the centre of Malta. With a population of about 25,000 people, it stands on an area of around 2.7 km^2. Today, Birkirkara is modern market town, buzzing with shoppers and despite this rapid business expansion, the town still retains its traditional feel characterised by the old alleyways, narrow streets and little houses full of character and charm.

There are many places of interest in Birkirkara, amongst them the Old Railway Station which is today located within a public garden. The quaint little single line track went from Valletta to Rabat but closed in 1931. Other town features include the Wignacourt Aqueduct built in the 17th Century, St Helen's Basilica, which has the distinction of having Malta's largest church bell, and the Ta'Ganu Windmill.

The windmill, built in 1724 by Manoel de Vilhena was in use until 1929. After World War II it was still serving as a blacksmith's workshop. In 1985/9 the building was restored, the stairs were rebuilt and water and electricity installed. In recent years a ceramist has been keeping the mill alive turning out his own work and exhibiting those of other artists.

The Parish Church, dedicated to St Helen, is a very fine example of baroque architecture and was built in 1727. It is a beautifully designed basilica and proudly houses the most famous bell in Malta which was installed around 1932. Another special feature in the church is the revered wooden statue of St Helen, which was completed in 1837 by the Maltese artist Salvu Psaila.

The main religious feast is that of St Helen which is celebrated each year on 18th August. The main event of the celebration is a procession with the large wooden statue of St Helen being carried through the town. This is a traditional procession and the only one in Malta which is carried out in the morning. The procession leaves the basilica at exactly 8:00 a.m. and returns to it at 10:45 a.m. The statue is carried shoulder-high by a group of townsmen and the whole population of Birkikara join in the celebration.

Birkirkara today continues to be a major town, with a myriad of small businesses and two industrial areas. Much of it is relatively modern but it still has a lot of old world charm especially in the area of St Helen's Church, which is defined by the traditional winding narrow streets and alleyways.

Tarxien

Tarxien is a town in the South Eastern Region of Malta with a population of about 8,000. The name of Tarxien is thought to have originated from the word "Tirix", which means a large stone and the motto of Tarxien is "Tyrii Genure Coloni" meaning "The Phoenicians created me".

 The town is widely known for the Tarxien Temples, a megalithic temple complex which are among the oldest freestanding structures in the world and forming part of a UNESCO World Heritage Site. The oldest temple here is said to date back to about 3600 BC. The temples feature various statues and reliefs of animals, including goats (for which Malta is noted) and pigs. Most interesting of the statues found in the Temples are about 2.5 metres in height, and are said to represent Mother Goddess or more specifically, Fertility. The parish of Tarxien is one of the oldest in Malta having been elevated to that status in 1592. The parish church is dedicated to the Annunciation of Our Lady and all the parishioners regard the Blessed

Virgin Mary, particularly her Annunciation, as the Patron and Protector of their town and its whole population.

A very important part of Tarxien culture is the feast of the Annunciation, which is celebrated in late May or the first Sunday of June. It is celebrated with many religious celebrations and liturgical services at the parish church, and throughout the town with street decorations, band marches and large aerial and ground firework displays.

The people of Tarxien are devout in their religious belief and practice it faithfully. In addition to their beautiful parish church, they also have a number of equally ornate smaller churches. The second largest church in town is dedicated to the Resurrection of Christ and it is used in conjunction with the old cemetery that surrounds it. This church is beside the renowned Tarxien Neolithic Temples and is visited by many tourists as many of the prehistoric remains were also found in the cemetery.

Other small chapels in Tarxien are two dedicated to St. Bartholomew and St. Mary respectively, another in the convent of the Sisters of Charity, dedicated to 'Our Lady of the Immaculate Conception', and the Augustinian's church of St Nicholas.

There is also another church dedicated to St. Nicholas of Tolentino and a convent which belongs to the Augustinian Friars.

Naxxar

Naxxar is one of those quaint old towns where life seems to be lived at a leisurely pace. Any time I passed through on a bus on my way to Valletta, I was fascinated to see lots of senior citizens sharing benches outside the Band Club enjoying a glass of tea while watching the world go by and the fruit and vegetable seller with his truck parked on a corner of the square greeting passers-by while waiting for the housewives to come with their shopping bags. The square seemed to be the assembly point for the town folk, where they would gather to relax and chat in the shadow of the majestic parish church, oblivious to the never-ending stream of passing traffic that continues to characterise the town centre.

It always fascinated me and when I eventually got around to visiting the town I found a quaint old town full of charm and warmth. Naxxar has something of historical, archaeological and cultural interest from each period in Malta's past. It has always been an important town and has played a role in major events in the Islands' history, from the arrival of Christianity to the defeat of the Ottoman Turks during the Great Siege of 1565. The town's name may derive from `nasra', meaning Christianity. St. Paul is said to have preached here after his shipwreck on the islands in AD 60. Naxxar's Latin motto translates as 'first to believe'.

Naxxar is a residential town spread over an area of 11 square kilometres (4 sq mi) and has a population of over eleven thousand people. It is built on a hill in the central-northern part of Malta, and is an old town, dating back to pre-historic times as cart ruts, Punic tombs and Catacombs have been discovered in various areas. There is much for the visitor to see in Naxxar including the Parish Church of Our Lady, one of the tallest baroque edifices on Malta, the church museum of processional statues, the town's many windmills, two round fortified towers, street niches, and the lavish Palazzo Parisio.

The Parish Church of Our Lady is the proud centrepiece of Nazzar. It was built between 1616 and 1630 and dominates the square with its sheer size and impressive facade. It was designed by Tumas Dingli, one of the best architects of the time and the church was solemnly consecrated by Bishop Alpheran de Bussan on 11th December 1732. The façade of the church has two clocks, one showing the actual time whilst the other is a painting and shows the time as a quarter to eleven (10.45).

The interior of the church is richly embellished; the main painting shows the Birth of Our Lady which is attributed to Mattia Preti (1613-1699) whilst at the side there are two paintings by Stefano Erardi (1650-1733) which shows the Flight to Egypt and the Adoration of the Magi. Other paintings which show the Madonna and Child, St Cajetan, St Aloysius Gonzaga, Our Saviour and Our Lady of Sorrows, are the work of the Maltese painter Frangisku Zahra (1680-1765). In the sacristy hangs the antique painting showing Our Lady of the Rosary which was painted on wood by Gio Maria Abela in 1595.

The main door, which is made of bronze, is dated 1913 and is the work of Pio Cellini. The door is made up of four main panels depicting the coat of arms of Our Lady, Patroness of Naxxar; the village coat of arms; the coat of arms of Pope St Pius X and the coat of arms of the family Zammit who were the benefactors of this door.

The Naxxar Festa is held on the 8th of September, in honour to Our Lady of Victory. The whole town is alive with activity during the week prior to the Festa. The Parish Church and the main streets are decorated in bright festive colours and people go out to the centre to listen to brass bands playing rousing music and watch the fireworks that fill the air with an exciting array of colours. On the streets, there are stalls selling local delicacies, such as candy floss and Nougat, the typical Maltese Festa sweet made out of sugar paste and nuts.

A big attraction for visitors to Naxxar is the lavish Palazzo Parisio. Located in a prominent spot in the square and built by a 19th century Maltese entrepreneur, Palazzo Parisio is a stately home unique in Malta. Its magnificent interior and baroque gardens have been described as a miniature Versailles. The Palazzo was acquired by the Marquis Scicluna in 1898. He embellished the building in the early 20th century, turning it into a palace. Palazzo Parisio and its gardens are in pristine condition and are now open to the public.

Palazzo Parisio's façade contains a large doorway flanked by a column on each side. The columns support an open balcony, and the latter's doorway contains the Scicluna coat of arms. The interior is richly decorated with frescoes, statues, columns, chandeliers and other works of art. The ballroom is gilded, and it is considered to be unique in Malta. The palace originally had very large gardens, but their size was reduced to make way for part of the former trade fair grounds. The Italian gardens near the palace still exist, and are now a big tourist attraction and a popular wedding venue.

There are many other interesting features of Naxxar to be explored on a stroll around this welcoming little town. I particularly like the trees and the greenery that adds special warmth to the town centre and I also enjoy wandering around the old parts, where several narrow streets and quaint houses make Naxxar a very charming and picturesque town.

Villages

For lovers of peace and old world charm like me, a stroll around Malta's villages is a joyful labour of love. They are hidden treasures and the epitome of Mediterranean character. Worlds away from the buzzing lifestyle of the big resorts and the busy towns, those little places are the heart and soul of the Islands. In their own inimitable way with their lively Festas and unique everyday life, they are very much part of the culture of today and yesterday. They all have their own proud centrepiece, the parish church, the landmark building usually visible from every corner of the village.

It is here that you will discover the unique character and the real heart of Malta. After visiting a few of those little villages you'll soon get the feeling of peace and tranquillity that pervades the narrow streets and quaint little squares, the serene and relaxed demeanour of the residents, and the general air of contentment that stays with you long after you have left.

Some villages are well known for their Festas and traditions; others are national treasures due to the presence of archaeological or architectural gems. There are also the seaside villages, where fishing is the way of life, while in inland villages the main activity is the harvesting of the various fruits and vegetables which are grown in little fields nearby.

Malta's villages come in all shapes and sizes. Some are tiny hamlets while others could almost be described as small towns. Having wondered about that, I discovered that a village is not defined by the number of residents or streets. The definition originated at a time when village boundaries were defined by parishes making it a bit difficult to see where the village ends and the hinterland begins. For us treasure hunters, the boundaries are not as important as the pleasure we get from the idyllic setting and quaint ambience of those hidden treasures that characterise the Maltese Islands and leave us visitors intrigued and inspired.

Mgarr

Mgarr is a small rural village surrounded by agricultural land, located in the northwest of Malta with a population of about 3,500 people. With its rich farmland and vineyards many of its inhabitants are farmers or are engaged in some sort of agricultural activity. The village is famous for the 'Festa Frawli' or the feast of strawberries. As the name suggests, during this particular event the locals showcases their strawberries.

Mġarr has two important prehistoric sites of worship. Ta Ħaġrat, which is still well preserved, stands in a field close to the town centre and Ta' Skorba, which was excavated in 1963, located just outside the village. This consists of two distinct temples which have been entered in the Guinness Book of Records as one of the two oldest free-standing structures in the world.

Mgarr's magnificent Parish Church stands majestically in the centre of the village on high ground and offers spectacular views of the surrounding countryside. The church is dedicated to Our Lady and has a unique oval dome that visitors always find intriguing. It is egg-shaped and one of the largest in Malta. Funds to build this church were collected from the sale of more than 300,000 eggs, and a huge number of poultry and animals. The villagers then dedicated the church to the Blessed Virgin and had the dome designed and constructed in the shape of an egg.

The Festa is celebrated on the Sunday following August 15th.

Mgarr is one of the parishes that organises an auction every year when parishioners bid an amount of money to carry the statue in the procession on the day of the Festa. In recent years the 'Festa Auction', as it is known in the village, raised up to €12,000. This old tradition dates back to 1923, when participants were asked to make a contribution to cover a deficit in the previous year's feast. The balance of the money then goes to a selected charity organisation.

Mgarr is a wonderful location for walkers and is invariably frequented by tourists who like to ramble and explore the green and fertile landscape. A walk down the steep hill leading from the square will lead you to the beach and the picturesque bay of Gnejna, with its colourful boat houses which serve as shelters from the summer heat for families on their beach excursions. The coastline around Mgarr extends from Fomm ir-Rih, a particularly beautiful, desolate spot to enjoy a swim in azure waters beneath steep cliffs. Further south is the more accessible Ghajn Tuffieha Bay with its golden sands. These pretty inlets were favourite sheltering places for pirates of old, and to protect the families living in Mgarr, Lippija Tower was built in 1657 by Grand Master Lascaris.

Like most Maltese, the inhabitants of Mgarr are devoted to their faith and religion. To protect themselves during the bombing raids of World War II, they constructed an underground air raid shelter in the village. It is beside the parish church and contains a miniature chapel where they prayed together even as bombs were falling overhead. This shelter is now open to visitors and is accessible from a restaurant called 'Il-Barri'.

The village of Mgarr is a must-visit gem. Although it is tiny, it is full of old world charm. The village centre has many little narrow streets with old houses adding to its beauty and character. I always feel welcome in this little village where the residents are friendly and welcoming, and always strive to live up to the village motto "small, with a big heart."

Attard

As I have already described Malta's three cities, Vittoriosa, Cospicua and Senglea, I will now take you to the island's three villages, Attard, Balzan and Lija. The villages are located in central Malta and all three adjoin each other. During the Golden Age of Malta, after the Great Siege, many noble families built homes here, and adorned the three villages with elegant villas and gardens.

Attard has a population of around 10,000 inhabitants and is the location for some important residents and organisations. As a municipality with its own local government structure since 1994, Attard covers an area of about seven square kilometres. To its north are the silent city of Mdina and also the flat expanse called Ta' Qali. Mdina is a huge tourist attraction but Ta'Qali is the home of some of Malta's highlights. Here is the Craft Village where the island's artists craft their beautiful handwork like glass, lace and the unique filigree jewellery. The National Stadium, the headquarters of Malta football, the Aviation Museum and the National Convention Centre are also housed in Ta'Qali.

It is also where the the President's official residence, San Anton Palace, is situated. Within walking distance of the President's residence is the official residence of the United States Ambassador to Malta. The Tunisian embassy to Malta is also located in Attard.

San Anton Palace is undoubtedly the most interesting attraction in Attard. It is not only rich in artistic and historical legacies, but has been a historical centre for entertainment and celebrations. The palace has greeted numerous royalties across the centuries, including Queen Marie of Romania, the Russian Empress Marie Feodorovna, King Edward VII and Queen Elizabeth II. It has seen the most distinguished visitors in contrasting personal situations - Napoleon's younger brother Louis Bonaparte as a prisoner and the poet Samuel Taylor Coleridge as an admiring recluse.

Governor Borton opened his botanic gardens to the public in 1882 for picnics and strolls. Its shaded open courtyards and gardens regularly host extremely popular fairs and competitions celebrating plants, flowers, animals and livestock. It also hosts music recitals, chamber orchestras and jazz concerts. During the Commonwealth Heads of Government Meeting in 2005, hosted by Malta, the President's Palace in Attard served as a residence for Queen Elizabeth II and Prince Philip.

The parish church of Attard is dedicated to the Assumption of the Blessed Virgin in Heaven and was built in 1613 by Tommaso Dingli. Like all the other villages in Malta, Attard has a big annual Festa and here the whole community celebrates the feast of the Assumption of Mary on 15 August. This date is a national holiday on the Maltese islands.

Attard's traditional Latin motto is *Florigera rosis halo* ("I perfume the air with my blossoms") due to its many flower gardens and citrus orchards. Attard is abundant with public gardens, including ornamental trees and flowers, maintained by the Local Council. Villa Bologna was the residence of the prime minister of Malta, Lord Strickland between 1927 and 1930. It is said to have the largest private garden in all of Malta and it is popular venue for weddings, fairs and parties.

Balzan

Balzan is another of the three villages located in central Malta. They are known as such because of their similar age, design, and because they merge into each other. Balzan shares its border with Attard and Lija and has a population of about 4,000 people. The village originally consisted of a group of small dwellings and farms but eventually grew to a parish in the 17th century.

As with Attard and Lija, Balzan is a location much sought after with the upper middle classes. The population has increased due to large-scale developments of apartment blocks replacing villas and gardens. However, this is mainly occurring on the outskirts, and the historic centre of the village remains intact and is an Urban Conservation Area.

Balzan got its name from Maximillian Balzan, a Spanish merchant who settled in Malta in 1567. For services rendered to the Knights of St John, he was given an area of land which later became the village of Balzan It was Maximillian who brought the lovely orange trees from Spain which now adorn the village.

Balzan is a quiet, peaceful village with a picturesque central square overlooked by the Parish Church of the Assumption. The church was built when the village became an independent parish in 1665 and is well worth a visit to see some beautiful paintings and statues by some of Malta's famous artists. The church is built in the form of a Latin cross, has one belfry and an elegant dome that can be seen from all around the village. It is built on a Tuscan style from the outside and Doric on the inside. The statue used in the village feast celebrated on the 2nd week of July, is carved in wood by Salvatore Dimech and shows Our Lady and Gabriel the Archangel.

Balzan is a lovely little village that I always like to visit and wander around in its relaxed atmosphere. Many of the traditional town houses still have back gardens full of lemon, orange and tangerine trees. Another delight found here is the citrus flavoured honey that comes from the hives in the area. In fact Balzan is well-known for its beautiful gardens and orchards of citrus fruits. It's not surprising that the motto of this picturesque village is Hortibus Undique Septa, meaning 'surrounded by gardens.'

Lija

Of the three villages in central Malta, Lija is definitely my favourite. If like me, you are in love with flowers, trees, gardens, and charming old world architecture, then this beautiful village will warm your heart. The main entrance into Lija is warm and welcoming. Lines of Oleander trees adorn Transfiguration Avenue, in the middle of which is the Belveder, a beautiful piece of architecture that used to form part of Villa Gourigion, the residence and gardens of Marquis Depiro. The village square is dominated by the impressive parish church which is dedicated to Our Savour. The old part of Lija is characterised by narrow winding streets, pretty alleys, beautiful baroque buildings and a tranquil feeling of peace and harmony. When I wander into this older part of the village, I am always charmed by the typical Maltese balconies, the cast-iron ornate windows holding geraniums of all colours, and homesteads adorned with corner niches, carved stone, timber balconies and iron railings.

Lija is a small village with a population of around 3,000 people. Like Balzan and Attard, it is noted for having large country residences, great gardens and orchards, and this gave Lija its motto 'Suavi Fructu Rubeo' which means, 'with tasty fruit I blossom'.

The village is famous for its fireworks displays that attract thousands of locals and tourists during the Festa held in the first week of August. These displays are renowned and claimed to be the best in Malta. The Lija fireworks team has won international fireworks competitions including an important one held in Monaco back in 1980.

The three little villages nestling in the heart of Malta are treasures to be explored and enjoyed. For many tourists they are hidden gems not yet discovered. I suggest that a day spent meandering around those exquisite little havens will fill you with a warm glow that will remain with you long after you have departed the shores of Malta.

Msida

Msida could be described now as a large village or a small town. It is located beside the harbour and has a population of 8,000 people. It was previously an old fishing village, but although it is now more urbanised, some fishermen still operate in the village. The lower part of Msida lies at the outlet of a valley and is mostly commercial. The higher part, which many tourists never see, is a charming old residential area with narrow hilly streets and winding pathways. Most of the lower village centre was reclaimed from the sea after the Second World War.

Today, Msida is best known and is hugely important for being the location of the University of Malta, the GF Abela Junior College, the Yacht Marina and the Mater Dei General Hospital.

The University overlooks the village from a hill known as Tal-Qroqq. There are 11,500 students on the campus, including 750 international students from 82 countries following full-time or part-time degree and diploma courses. Over 3,000 students graduate annually. There are a further 2,500 students at the Junior College, which is also managed by the university. Most of the students commute daily but those from Gozo and the international students are accommodated in the surrounding areas. All this movement of lively and exuberant young people creates a buzz around Msida in stark contrast to Malta's other quieter and more tranquil inland villages.

The Msida and Ta' Xbiex Marinas, many times referred to as the Sliema Marina, form the largest marina in Malta. These Marinas together provide mooring facilities for more than 700 boats on 15 serviced pontoons. It is located inside Marsamxett Harbour, which makes it safe and well sheltered, as well as conveniently central. The Marina is operated by Creek Developments Plc, who provides every facility, including showers, toilets, water and electricity.

The Marina can handle pleasure yachts of up to 22 metres in length at this excellent picturesque location. I have often strolled around this expansive enclosure of luxury which is always full to capacity with gorgeous yachts of all shapes and sizes. I find it an absorbing experience and a fleeting glimpse of another world.

The Mater Dei is Malta's new state of the art hospital and is situated on the outskirts of Msida. Opened in 2007, it is the flagship of the excellent health services of the Maltese Islands. It is massive, covering 250,000 square metres and commands a strategic position visible from far and wide. Some of its statistics are staggering; 3,760 staff, 850 beds, 25 fully equipped operating theatres and cost 600 million Euro to build. It was a brave move by the Malta government to embark on such an ambitious project but now their vision and courage is much appreciated by everyone who needs its services, including many tourists.

As in most Malta villages the dominant landmark is the parish church and Msida is another example of the pride and status of the church in its midst. Saint Joseph's Parish Church stands tall and elegant in the centre of the village and is clearly visible from every direction. It is a beautiful traditional baroque design, built in the late 19th century and replaced the old church of the Immaculate Conception which still exists today.

The façade is hugely impressive comprising of a series of bays with the two outer bays surmounted by well-proportioned bell-towers. However, the main artistic highlight lies within the interior of the church with a mystical fresco painting over the choir vault depicting the death of St Joseph. Msida's Festa in honour of St Joseph is quite special because it is celebrated for a full week and a half in July. It is also unique for the playing of the traditional game known as il-Gostra (pronounced il-jostra) where local men compete in trying to reach a flag at the end of a slippery log and invariably splash into the sea below!

Most tourists only get a passing glance of Msida when travelling between Valletta, Sliema and other towns and resorts. But having spent many enjoyable days in and around Msida I can say it is a bustling, lively and stimulating area, well worth spending a few hours there and exploring its many interesting features.

Zebbug

Żebbuġ, also known in Maltese as Citta Rohan, is a small town in the Southern Region of Malta. It is one of the oldest towns in the country, and its population is 12,000 people. It was given the title of Città Rohan by Grandmaster Emmanuel de Rohan-Polduc in 1777. On such occasions, it was the custom for the inhabitants to build a gate to serve as an entrance to the town. The big ornate structure was duly built and it still stands at the town's entrance today. Approaching Zebbug from the direction of Valletta visitors are welcomed by this most striking architectural feature of the town, the de Rohan Arch.

In olden times the town had lots of olive trees growing around the central square and so the name of the town became Zebbug which in Maltese means olives. When Malta was ruled by the Knights of St John, Żebbuġ was a key town and was held next in importance to Valletta and Mdina. This was primarily because of high ranking dignitaries who lived here and also because of the thriving cotton industry. The splendour of St. Philip's Church is the prime symbol of importance of Żebbuġ in Maltese history. Many prehistoric remains have been found around the area such as pottery, Punic and Phoenician tombs and a number of those intriguing cart ruts which archaeologists have never managed to agree as to their true origin.

When in Zebbug you must visit the majestic parish church dedicated to St Philip of Agira, which was built in 1380 and is truly a museum of art. There you will find a magnificent titular painting by Luca Garnier, which is hugely acclaimed. You will also see the famous statue of the much-loved patron, St Philip, which was created in 1864 and is considered to be a masterpiece.

The annual village Festa in honour of St Philip, which is celebrated on the second Sunday of June, is regarded as one of the best in Malta. For several days three competing band clubs, fireworks factories and all the fun and flair typical of a Maltese village Festa is enjoyed by locals and visitors. Zebbug is also well-known for having one of the best Good Friday pageants on the islands.

Siggiewi

Siġġiewi village stands on a plateau overlooking a landscape of fertile agricultural land in southwest Malta not far from the picturesque coastline of Dingli Cliffs. It is a most attractive area and this typical Maltese countryside is home to some charming little hamlets such as Fawwara and some small wayside chapels such as the miniature baroque Tal-Provvidenza, just outside the main village.

The village is about 10km from Valletta and is quite near to the old silent city of Mdina. It has a population of around 9000 people, most of whom were farmers traditionally working in the fields that surround the village. Siggiewi is an old village established in the 14th century, and on December 30th 1797 it was promoted to 'city' status by the Grandmaster Ferdinand Von Hompesch who christened it "Città Ferdinand".

The most striking feature of the village of Siggiewi is the spectacular perspective of the central square. The monument of its patron saint, St Nicholas of Bari, is the focal point, set against the imposing baroque facade of the parish church, which is dedicated to the same saint. The money to build the church was raised by the villagers themselves between 1676 and 1693 and the church was designed by Lorenzo Gafa', the designer of Mdina Cathedral. St. Nicholas Parish Church is one of the finest examples of a baroque parish church. Its massive dome, dominating the skyline for miles around, and the impressive facade, are late 19th century additions by local architect Nicholas Zammit. The square in front of the church is remarkable for its size, its two chapels and the huge shrine of St. Nicholas.

Mattia Preti added his contribution to this beautiful church with a large altarpiece, 'The Miracle of St Nicholas,' where the Saint is portrayed saving a child kidnapped by the Saracens. The Saint holds the child by the scalp and transports him heavenward, later to return him to his family. The depiction of this miracle doubtlessly touched the hearts of the Maltese population, as they had been regularly attacked by Saracen pirates over the centuries.

The area around Siggiewi is ideal for walking tours. From the village you can easily reach Ghar Lapsi, This beauty spot and popular bathing place is perhaps one of the must-visit delights of Siggiewi, with its cave and natural sea-pool of crystal green and blue waters. A walk along the cliffs is also enjoyable and refreshing providing beautiful sea views especially the little Islet of Filfla.

A visit to Siggiewi during the Festa of St Nicholas is an unforgettable experience. It is held the last Sunday in June, although the festivities are actually going on for a whole week. This is the traditional Maltese Festa with the magnificent Church of Saint-Nicolas of Bari beautifully decorated and lit up, the village in full colour celebrating with the music of brass bands, processions and fireworks.

Siggiewi is another of Malta's hidden treasures, a charming old village full of character surrounded by little green fields and beautiful old rustic farmhouses. As you walk through the old part of the village, you find some delightful old homesteads with the niches, some of which date from the 17th century. It is truly the heart and soul of Malta.

Luqa

Luqa is a village located in the south east of Malta. It is old and densely populated with a total of 6,000 residents. For many centuries it was a typically quiet Malta village.

In the 1920s when the island was a British colony an airstrip for military use was constructed on land outside the village. Later, when the airstrip was developed to accommodate passenger airlines, the area of Luqa became synonymous with what is now Malta International Airport.

The airport was completely re-furbished, becoming fully operational on 25th March 1992. It is now an important international airport hosting many of the world's top airlines including the Maltese national airline, Air Malta. It has grown substantially over the recent years and its healthy statistics for 2015 were, Passengers 4,618,642, Aircraft Movements 34,283, Cargo Movements 14,964,462 KG. On the many occasions that I use the airport I always enjoy the experience. The services and facilities are excellent and the workers there are always warm and friendly.

The presence of the airport meant that Luqa had to endure many serious air raids during World War II and the village was almost completely devastated. The Parish Church dedicated to St Andrew, a masterpiece of art and architecture which also houses the titular painting by Mattia Preti (1687), was originally built in 1670 but due to heavy war damage had to be totally reconstructed between 1944 and 1962.

However, some of the important landmarks we find in Luqa today have survived since the pre-war period. The construction of the airport and modern development also served to uncover several ancient tombs, human remains and artefacts in the area, from Roman remains to other prehistoric remains which date back to the Bronze Age. Visitors to Luqa rarely leave without seeing the old dwelling house of the famous clock maker and inventor Michelangelo Sapiano, who lived in Pawlu Magri Street from 1826 to1912. His work can be seen in the beautiful clock that adorns the belfry of the Parish Church. The wayside chapel dedicated to St. James (1550) is also a little gem of the village.

There are two band clubs in Luqa and every year on the feast of St Andrew in July the Union Band Club and St Andrew's Band Club are centre stage for the Village Festa. Luqa is lavishly decorated for the occasion, creating a carnival atmosphere during the Festa and an eager anticipation for the community throughout the weeks leading up to it.

Paola

A small town in the South Eastern Region of Malta, Paola has a population of 8,000 people. It is named after Grand Master Antoine de Paule who laid the foundation stone in 1626. A modern urban area on the hill overlooking Grand Harbour, Paola shares a common past with Valletta. It too is a new town, designed by the Knights on a grid system like that of the capital city. The plan, devised by Grand Master de Paule, was for the town to serve as a summer resort taking advantage of the cooler breezes offered by its hilltop location. It was not until the mid-to-late 19th century that Paola really grew and the town's population rose rapidly once the nearby dockyards expanded.

Paola today has two parish churches, one dedicated to Christ the King and the other to Our Lady of Lourdes. The Church of Christ the King was completed in 1959 and area-wise is the largest church in Malta. It stands in the main square and dominates the town centre. The feast of Christ the King is celebrated on the fourth Sunday of July and Our Lady of Lourdes is celebrated on the first Sunday after 17th August.

Within Paola's tight grid of streets lies Malta's most precious prehistoric site: the Hypogeum underground burial chambers and temple, a UNESCO World Heritage Site. For the throngs of visitors who come every year, exploring this underground burial site, carved out into the rock more than 5000 years ago, is one of their most memorable and inspiring experiences. Walking down the labyrinthine structure of chambers, adorned with red figures and spirals, deep into a profound silence, can feel like going into the womb of Mother Earth.

This extraordinary necropolis was discovered by a stonemason in 1902, and contained the remains of over 7000 people in addition to the artefacts of their former lives, including amulets, beads, pottery, carved animals and figurines. The most exquisite of the figurines found was the enchanting 'Sleeping Lady', of which the original is on exhibit in the National Museum of Archaeology in Valletta.

Fgura

Fgura is a lovely small residential and commercial town in South Malta. It has developed in recent years to a densely populated area from just a handful of little farms that existed there before the Second World War. It is now a modern, self-sufficient town of 12,000 inhabitants, with spacious roads, a number of public squares and gardens and a myriad of shops and commercial premises.

Much of Fgura was built around the 1960s and 1980s. However, the town has prehistoric roots - there are several tombs in the area - and there is evidence to suggest it was a settlement in Phoenician times. Fgura, located inland from the Three Cities, was influenced by the growth of the dockyards, especially after World War II. Its northern fringes are bordered by the Cottoner Lines of fortifications, while it merges with the towns of Żabbar to the south and Tarxien to the West.

There is evidence that where the town now stands a settlement existed in Phoenician times. In 1948, six Phoenician tombs were found in Fgura, dating to the 3rd or 4th century B.C. These tombs were in irregular shapes and human skeletons, remains of animals, pottery and other Bronze materials and objects were found. To commemorate this historic finding, a street in the town was named 'Triq is-Sejba Punika' which in English means: 'Phoenician Discovery Street'.

Patron saint of Fgura is Our Lady of Mount Carmel and an annual feast in her honour is celebrated on the second Sunday of July. Fgura has one of the most peculiar shaped churches in Malta and is in total contrast to the traditional baroque churches seen in almost every town and village. It is built in the shape of a tent but in its own way is one of the most beautiful little churches on the Island. After the Second World War, the Carmelite Fathers were entrusted with the spiritual needs of the community. They arrived in Fgura in 1945, and proceeded to build a new church and convent, which were inaugurated in November 1950.

Although the entire town of Fgura is relatively modern with some lovely ornate squares and interesting monuments, there are also parts of the town that are old and original. One of the oldest streets in Fgura is Triq il-Karmnu (Carmel Street), which was originally a short cut from Bulebel to Zabbar, bypassing Paola. This quaint little street is still dotted with some of the original farmhouses and conveys a feeling of history and old world charm.

Zabbar

Żabbar, also known as Città Hompesch, is a town in the South Eastern Region of Malta. It is a town with a great historical and architectural heritage and has a population of 15,000 residents. When approaching Żabbar from Paola, visitors are greeted by a large impressive arch located on the main road at the entrance to the town. This was erected by the residents to mark the occasion in 1797 when Żabbar was given the title of Città Hompesch by the Grandmaster Ferdinand von Hompesch zu Bolheim,

Żabbar's history goes back to the Great Siege in 1565 when the area was used as a camp by the Ottoman armies. It was also used as a base by the Maltese when they rose against the French around 1800. Cannon balls from this era can still be seen in walls in the older parts of the town and some cannon balls which were recovered from the old church's dome are now displayed in the church museum.

The impressive Parish Church dominates this typical large Maltese village. It is dedicated to Our Lady of Graces and was built in 1660. The church has been redesigned and embellished over the years, with two bell towers erected, the church paved in marble, and a new crypt built. It is now a magnificent church, its grandeur reflecting the devotion and pride of the people of Żabbar, who continued to embellish their church using their own funds. This architectural gem is richly decorated, with a main painting of the Madonna and Child by Alessio Erardi, while a famous painting by Mattia Preti is on display in the adjoining Sanctuary Museum. VFGA - a Latin abbreviation for Votum Fecit, Gratiam Accipit - is imprinted on many of the paintings and artefacts found in the Sanctuary Museum, which refers to the graces granted due to the intercession of the Madonna tal-Grazzja (Our Lady of Graces) to whom the parishioners pray faithfully to this day.

Zabbar celebrates two feasts, one held for Our Lady of Graces on the first Sunday after 8th September, and one held in honour of St. Michael the Archangel two weeks later. The former is famous for its motorcycle and bicycle pilgrimage, starting from Mosta and Rabat respectively. This is to honour the legend that Our Lady of Graces is the patron of cyclists. The cultural rivalry between the village's two band clubs, the Società Filarmonica Maria Mater Gratiæ (the Blues) and the Ghaqda Madonna Tal-Grazzja Banda San Mikiel (the Greens) is highlighted during these Festas but also adds greatly to the colour and vibrancy of the occasions.

The town of Zabbar made international news in 1975 when a Vulcan air-plane crashed on to the main street hitting a school, killing five members of the crew and one resident. The fact that no children were lost was considered nothing short of a miracle since the students were not in the school when the plane crashed and the villagers have been thanking their patron il-Madonna tal-Grazzja ever since. A number of items from this episode, including the aircraft undercarriage, can still be seen at the Zabbar Sanctuary Museum. This museum has also a number of important paintings and other artefacts including a precious painting by the famous Mattia Preti.

Qormi

This town in the Southern Region of Malta is located southwest of Valletta. It has a population of 16,000 with residential and light industrial areas, but the town's core is still characterised by alleys and narrow streets. Because of its low-lying position near Grand Harbour, Qormi played a distinct role throughout its history. The town traditionally provided a workforce of stevedores for the harbour and became the first place where imported goods were stored. Wheat was one of the staple imports. Over the years, windmills sprang up in the town and it soon developed a thriving break-making industry. Qormi has been known as the centre of bread-making in Malta since the time of the Knights of St. John. It became known as 'the bakers' village, as it is still known today.

Qormi has two parishes, dedicated to Saint George and Saint Sebastian. Saint George's parish was the first one. However, when Qormi was growing, there was the need for the town to be split into two parishes to facilitate growth. Saint Sebastian was chosen because Qormi had turned to him during times of plague infestation, since he is the protector and patron saint of people ill from plague, according to Catholic tradition. This led to many Qormi citizens carrying the name of *Ġorġ* (George) and *Bastjan* (Sebastian).

The Church of Saint George, with its elegant facade and imposing dome, is home to the last work that Preti painted: 'St George the Martyr', located on the main altar. The Saint, shown while being beheaded, is illuminated by the divine light. Though many of the paintings were executed by his workshop, it is believed that Preti, seriously ill and soon to die, still found the energy to add his final brushstrokes to this masterpiece. This painting also contains a curious detail; in the background one can see a young St George on horseback in the act of killing the dragon to save the princess.

The subject matter is the same as one of the early paintings that Preti executed in Malta, on display by the altar in the Chapel of the Langue of Aragon in St John's Co-cathedral in Valletta. The town's second parish church, the Church of St. Sebastian, completed in the 1980s, is in neo-Romanesque style and carries a distinctive huge, white dome. The Festa of St George is celebrated on the last Sunday in June and the Festa in honour of St. Sebastian is celebrated every third Sunday of July. On Easter Sunday every year a procession is held with the tradition of running with the statue of the Risen Christ along various roads throughout the town and is a special occasion in the parish.

Beaches and Bays

Malta has lots of beaches of various kinds, some ideal for bathing, others suitable for windsurfers and snorkelling. There are little beaches and inlets with golden sand, some with red sand, pebble beaches, rocks, blue lagoons and even inland seas. Some beaches and rocky shores are hidden away, but are well worth seeking out for their seclusion. The most famous of all is Comino's Blue Lagoon, worth taking the boat trip for the ultimate in azure water.

Most beaches have cafes or snack bars open during the summer season and given Malta's excellent climate, beach life lasts well into October. Water sports and other activities like windsurfing, jet and water skiing are well catered for, with equipment available to hire from beach cafes or shops nearby.

The northern part of Malta is where the larger sandy beaches and the most popular coastal resorts are located. Mellieħa Bay, Għajn Tuffieħa and Golden Bay are all found here and also some smaller inlets such as Paradise Bay and Armier. Because Malta is such a small island, the nearest swimming spot is never more than a ten minute drive away. Some of the larger sandy beaches can get a bit overcrowded in summer but there are plenty of lesser-known spots where many visitors frequent and enjoy a lovely swim in quiet seclusion.

Mistra Bay

Mistra Bay is a beautiful secluded little bay frequented more by the Maltese than tourists. It is reached by a detour off the main road leading from Xemxija to Mellieha. The Bay is set in one of Malta's most green and fertile areas with little fields and vegetable crops stretching along both sides of the approach road. The pebble beach is small and quaint and in summer is a popular hide-away for Maltese who come and bask in the hot sun in little tents on the beach.

Mistra Bay is unspoiled with no development or commercial activity. But there is a good restaurant located just across the road from the bay. Out at sea and visible from the bay are some fish farming pens which are part of a growing lucrative industry off the island. During the winter months the little bay is almost deserted but that is when I like to ramble down there. I then have this idyllic little haven all to myself and I can enjoy the peace and solitude, and sense time standing still.

Paradise Bay

Paradise Bay is a sandy beach at the northernmost tip of the island, close to the quay where the two ships operate a shuttle service daily to Gozo. This little beach is a quiet spot that offers tranquillity and seclusion despite its proximity to a busy environment in the distance. The beach also offers a good view of the island of Comino with its imposing tower. It is part of the Paradise Bay Hotel but open to the public as well as for hotel residents. The water is crystal clear and ideal for family relaxation.

Paradise Bay is one of the most popular beaches in Malta due to its natural environment and clear waters and won a 'Beach of Quality' award in 2012. It offers beautiful views of the surrounding rugged landscape, over Malta's sister Islands Gozo and Comino, and over the beautiful blue Mediterranean Sea.

Pretty Bay

Pretty Bay is one of the few sandy beaches in the southern region of Malta. It is located in the town of Birżebbuġa - a small seaside resort not far from Marsaxlokk in southeast Malta. It has been a popular bathing spot for Maltese holiday-makers for decades.

Originally a rocky coast where up to some years ago, sand was virtually non-existent, the bay was artificially filled with sand recovered from the sea during dredging works for a nearby project. Pretty Bay is now one of the prettiest sandy beaches on the island. It lies right in the town centre where there are plenty of shops and restaurants.

Always bustling with activity, the bay offers something for everyone including beach sport activities and windsurfing. A number of restaurants, bars, cafes, shops and kiosks line the street opposite the beach. There is also a rocky area situated only a few minutes' walk outside Pretty Bay which makes it an ideal spot for snorkelling.

St George's Bay

St. George's Bay is a very popular sandy beach located in Paceville, St Julian's, close to many hotels, restaurants and the entertainment centre of Malta. The bay saw major positive development and improvements over the years, which has made this a very popular little beach resort. As it is located in the entertainment capital of Malta and is surrounded by many hotels and language schools, it can get very crowded with tourists during summer and is especially popular during the night, when crowds of young people gather to socialize.

St George's Bay is a picturesque and pleasant little resort. It has a feeling of quaintness despite its proximity to one of Malta's liveliest urban areas renowned for its nightlife activity. Facilities and services are excellent with plenty of restaurants, bars and shopping centres. Another big plus for swimmers and sun-seekers is that St George's Bay is a 'Blue Flag Beach.'

Golden Bay

This is one of Malta's most popular sandy beaches set within a cliff face in the North West and it is one of a chain of beaches in that area. It is relatively undeveloped and has easy access for the less mobile or those with small children. Golden Bay has excellent facilities; a cafe-restaurant, sun lounges and umbrella hire, and plenty of fun water sports from jet skiing and paragliding to banana boat rides. The spectacular sunsets here make the beach a popular spot for evening barbecues. Golden Bay is located along unspoiled and undeveloped countryside and the blue sea and cliffs surrounding the bay provide excellent snorkelling.

Beach management is operated by the Malta Tourism Authority from 15th June to 15th September. Lifeguards and other beach staff are present daily during this period. The beach is generally safe for swimming but it is prone to strong currents when the wind is to the north-west. When the red flag is signalled, bathing is limited to shallow waters due to underwater currents from the North West winds.

The Radisson Golden Sands Hotel dominates the cliff-top and provides fine accommodation and excellent dining facilities. Golden Bay is a large beach with beautiful waters and spectacular views, making it the second most popular beach in Malta after Mellieha Bay.

Għajn Tuffieħa

Għajn Tuffieħa Bay is one of three beautiful, sandy beaches on the north-western coast of Malta, with the other two being Golden Bay and Gnejna Bay. It is a picturesque and unspoilt beach with fine reddish sand. The beach is smaller than Golden Bay, is set in idyllic surroundings with a hillside behind which is designated a national park. The foundation managing the hillside has planted tamarisk and samphire to prevent further erosion at this beautiful natural bay.

Għajn Tuffieħa's location and the fact that it is accessed by a flight of steps means it is not usually as crowded as its neighbour, but its fine sand and rural atmosphere make it more alluring. The beach is generally safe for swimming but it is prone to strong currents when the wind is to the north-west. A red flag indicates when bathing should be limited to the shallow waters.

Beach management includes the services of a lifeguard and safety ropes affixed along the bay. The beach was awarded a 'Beach of Quality' award for 2012. This is a charming little hidden heaven especially for those that linger on after most bathers leave for home and enjoy the best time on the beach - the spectacular sunsets.

Anchor Bay

Anchor Bay is one of the most popular beaches in Malta, famous mainly as a diving site, but especially for Popeye Village. It is a gorgeous little inlet with beautiful green-blue clear water that is surrounded by rocky hills. Located about one kilometre west of the village of Mellieha in northern Malta, it is a major attraction for tourists who flock to see Popeye Village where the whole set of Sweetheaven Village, the film starring Robin Williams as Popeye, still stands intact as it did when filming in 1979. The film set is today a theme park and an activity centre attracting mainly families with young children.

Located between two cliffs, Anchor Bay is also popular for its stunning caves and beautiful underwater sea life that make this secluded bay a prime spot for snorkelers and divers alike. On the left side of the bay, there is a cave known as Scorpion Cave. Its entrance is completely submerged for the first few meters. Snorkelers can use another entrance to enjoy the stunning views inside the cave.

Divers at the other side of the bay will find a large anchor with an enormous chain which gave the name to this bay. Old anchors which have been found here are on display at the Maritime Museum in Vittoriosa. The bay offers explorers of the underwater life an opportunity to see a lot of fish including scorpion fish, morays, groupers, parrot fish and octopus. The bay itself is quite secluded and is therefore less frequented by swimmers. Although the water is beautifully clear and adequate for swimming, it is mainly a diving location because of its several caves.

Armier Bay

Located in a rural area, Armier Bay is home to beautiful azure crystal waters. The beach stretches around the shore of an open bay at the extreme northern fringe of Malta. It is in the locality of Mellieha and is actually two beaches with the biggest beach known as Armier and the other one known as Little Armier. Situated opposite of Comino, the bay benefits from crystal clear waters like the Blue Lagoon.

Armier Bay is home to several boat houses mostly utilised by locals as summer residences. Being a rural area, no hotels are available nearby, but facilities such as bars, quaint restaurants and water sports operators are all available whilst also making the area an ideal and popular area for barbeques.

During summer, Armier Bay can sometimes get very busy especially at weekends. However, the Armier beaches are usually quieter than other beaches since they are not as accessible and there is no big influx of tourists from nearby hotels. Since both Armier Bay and Little Armier are located near Mellieha in a beautiful countryside landscape, the area makes a wonderful and prime location for long walks during winter.

Mellieha Bay

Mellieha Bay, also known as Ghadira Bay, is the largest and one of the most beautiful sandy beaches in the Maltese Islands. It is a sheltered beach between two headlands and is situated in the Northern part of the Island. The shallow water that is ankle deep for about 50 metres out to sea and easy accessibility, makes the beach one of the most family friendly beaches in Malta. Idyllic and scenic, the resort is only one mile away from the quaint village of Mellieha which sits on top of a hill.

Renowned for its beautiful long sandy beach, fine sand and shallow waters that stretch out for a mile, Mellieha Bay is the perfect destination for families and those who prefer to relax on the beach. There are endless activities **to** choose from like windsurfing, kite surfing, canoeing and water-skiing.

Mellieħa Bay has lots of facilities and services including restaurants and two hotels. Some parts of the bay area are designated for water sports and wind surfing. Beach management is operated between June and September by the Malta Tourism Authority with the co-operation of Mellieħa Local Council. It includes the services of lifeguards, a small First Aid clinic, two beach supervisors and a number of persons in charge of beach maintenance. Even though Mellieħa Bay is the most popular sandy beach in Malta, it is large enough not to be too crowded, except during weekends in the peak summer months.

Mellieħa Bay does not have any underwater currents and hardly ever experiences rough seas, making the Bay ideal and safe for swimmers of all ages. It is an easy accessible beach furnished with toilets, wheelchair access and special sand wheelchair buggies for physically impaired bathers. In 2011, the beach was awarded a 'Beach of Quality Award.'

Mellieħa Bay has an old castle perched on one side, while the old village of Mellieħa is situated high on the opposite side. The hinterland of Mellieħa Bay was once an important salt flat and wetland, known as L-Għadira. It is now a Nature Reserve that boasts of indigenous flora and fauna, and is popular with bird watchers who study local and migratory birds.

World War II

The most documented period of Malta's history is the Second World War. The Islands' strategic location once again made it centre stage in the theatre of war in the Mediterranean; a key stronghold from which the Allies could sustain their North African campaign and from which they could launch their eventual attack on mainland Italy.

Before that happened though, the Islands were subject to some of the most severe bombardments of the entire war. The Maltese people may have ended the war with the distinction of being the only entire population to be awarded the George Cross, Britain's highest civilian honour for bravery, but they also ended the war devastated. Malta holds the record for the heaviest, sustained bombing attack; some 154 days and nights and 6,700 tons of bombs.

In 1943, Malta was one of the launch pads for the Allied invasion of Sicily and later, the push into Italy. The Italian navy surrendered on the 8th of September, by coincidence the very same day on which 378 years earlier, the Great Siege had ended.

The end of the war saw the Islands economically and physically devastated. In 1947, they were granted some £30 million to help rebuild. But it took several decades and further restructuring once the British forces left Malta completely in 1979, to rebuild the economy.

Memorials

The Malta Memorial

Due to its pivotal contribution to the war in the Mediterranean, Malta was the chosen location of the memorial to the 2,298 Commonwealth aircrew who lost their lives in the various Second World War air battles and engagements around the Mediterranean, and who have no known graves. Built on land generously donated by the Government of Malta, the Malta Memorial is located in the area of Floriana, to the south side of the Triton Fountain close to City Gate, the entrance to Valletta. It was inaugurated by Queen

Elizabeth II on 3rd of May 1954. The memorial is identified by the gilded bronze golden eagle which surmounts the 49 ft column of Travertine marble. The column stands on a circular base around which the names are inscribed on bronze panels.

The Malta Memorial is an impressive landmark clearly visible as one enters Valletta and is a fitting memorial to all those brave men who gave their lives in the fight for freedom.

The Siege Bell

The monument was designed by Michael Sandle, a prolific and important sculptor worldwide and assembled on the initiative of the George Cross Island Association to commemorate the 50th anniversary of the presentation of this award to Malta. The Valletta Rehabilitation Project, under the leadership of its chief executive officer and coordinator Ray Bondin, was responsible for its construction.

The surrounding landscape is part of the Castille bastion underlying the Lower Barakka Gardens. The site was specifically chosen because it marks the furthermost point of Valletta within the Grand Harbour and is secluded to complement the meditating nature of the scope of the monument while the bell tolls solemnly in commemoration of the fallen heroes.

The design of the structure consists of a belfry in the form of an elliptical neo classical temple supported by ten square-faced columns. The colonnaded belfry contains a huge bourdon bell which is the largest bell in Malta.

The columns rise from a high base designed on the plan inspired from the form of the George Cross. Further from the belfry a bronze catafalque symbolising the burial of the corpse of the Unknown Soldier at sea, overhangs the bastion parapet. The inspiration of the monument is based on the Maria Gloriosa mediaeval bourdon bell of Erfurt Cathedral in Germany. The tolling bourdon bell was intended to build up a drone, its tone solemnly lamenting the demise of the heroes across the waves of Grand Harbour.

The bell was cast on February the 10th, 1992, by the world's largest bell founders John Taylor & Co. Founders, of Loughborough England. A Latin inscription adorning the bell stating a verse in Latin translates to "You cast thy shadow upon my head during the time of war 1940-1943".

Aviation Museum

Malta Aviation Museum is an aircraft museum situated on the site of the former Royal Air Force airfield in the village of Ta'Qali. The museum, based in three hangars, covers the history of aviation on the island with exhibits from the Second World War and post-war periods. The museum is involved in the preservation and restoration of exhibits, some to airworthy condition. The location of the museum is most appropriate being on the old airfield of Takali (Ta'Qali), Malta's first civilian airport, opened in 1938, which, during WW II became a fighter airfield, gaining the distinction of being the most bombed airfield in the world.

This is another must-see hidden treasure especially for visitors like me with a keen interest in aviation or in the history of World War 11, and Malta's heroic defence of the skies. The island's heavy participation and air bombardment have left a significant number of aircraft relics on the island and around its Mediterranean waters. The aircrafts' salvage and restoration has been the focus of a dedicated and passionate team that run this non-profit organisation. The Malta Aviation Museum Foundation, made up mostly of volunteers, continuously strives to acquire new items for display in its collection to enhance the island's rich aviation history.

The Museum's collection comprises of wartime aircraft and post war jets, including the well-known Supermarine Spitfire Mk IX, Hawker Hurricane IIa, de Havilland Tiger Moth, North American T6 Texan, Douglas Dakota IV, as well as a Fairey Swordfish, Beechcraft 18 and others. The jets consist of de Havilland Vampire T11, Hawker Seahawk, Fiat G91R and Gloster Meteors T7, F8 and NF14. Aircraft engines, airfield vehicles and equipment, uniforms and memorabilia are also displayed.

The Malta Aviation Museum is an interesting attraction for both local and overseas tourists. It is also an ideal family attraction guaranteed to captivate visitors even if they are not aviation enthusiasts.

Lascaris War Rooms

The Lascaris War Rooms are an underground complex of tunnels and chambers that served as the War Headquarters from where the defence of Malta was conducted during the Second World War. The underground War Rooms, hidden away 400 feet under the Upper Barrakka Gardens, were the Mediterranean World War II Headquarters of the Allied Forces operations, are one of the unique secrets of Valletta, and an intriguing attraction of which only a handful exist worldwide.

This top secret complex contained an operations room for each of the fighting services which included the vital RAF Fighter Control Room from where all air and sea operations were observed and controlled. Supporting it was a Filter Room through which was channelled and filtered all radar traffic, as well as an Anti-aircraft Gun Operations Room from where artillery fire was co-ordinated. There was also a large combined operations room for all three services, additional administrative rooms, and (hidden from most military staff due to its secrecy) the Cypher Rooms. Code and encryption machines were kept in the Cypher Rooms to send and receive all secret communications to and from Malta. Being so deep underground, the whole complex was mechanically ventilated; one of the original features that still works today.

In July 1943, the War Rooms were used by General Eisenhower and his Supreme Commanders, Admiral Cunningham, Field Marshal Montgomery and Air Marshal Tedder as their advanced Allied HQ for Operation Husky – the invasion of Sicily. This complex continued in military use throughout the Cold War until 1977, just two years before the closure of the British base in 1979.

After the war, the Lascaris War Rooms became the Mediterranean Fleet Headquarters, playing an important role in the Anglo-French invasion of Egypt during the Suez crisis in 1956, and going into full alert for a number of days during the Cuban Missile Crises of 1962. In 1967 it was taken over by NATO to be used as a strategic Communication Centre for the interception of Soviet submarines in the Mediterranean. After 10 years in this role the rooms were eventually closed down.

The Lascaris War Rooms are a great attraction just a short walk from the centre of Valletta. They have been recently and expertly restored by Fondazzjoni Wirt Artna (an NGO entrusted with a number of priceless heritage attractions on the islands). In 2009, the Malta Heritage Trust undertook the challenging task of restoring this historic complex. As a result of this work visitors can now explore and enjoy one of Malta's best kept wartime secrets. The Lascaris War Rooms is the first major part completed of a grand project being undertaken to create a Military Heritage Park that will also comprise many other attractions in the vicinity. Tours are conducted in English but multilingual audio tapes are also available.

Malta at War Museum

The 'Malta at War Museum' is located at Couvre Porte, Vittoriosa (Birgu). It stands to document the great ordeal which the brave people of Malta and their defenders endured during the dark days of the Malta Blitz (1940-43) in World War 11.

Vittoriosa is Malta's old maritime city, first convent of the Knights of St. John before Valletta (1530), Great Siege Headquarters (1565) and former home to the Royal Navy (1800 – 1979). Ensconced within Dockyard Creek, it inevitably became one of the worst bombed places of the war with almost half of it being destroyed as a result of enemy bombing. The museum is housed in an 18th century army barracks which served as a police station and air raid precautions centre during the war. It sits on top of a massive underground rock-cut air raid shelter which offered refuge to hundreds of people. This shelter has been restored and forms part of the museum experience.

At this museum, one can also watch the first documentary ever made on the island 'Malta G.C.' This short film was released by the Crown Film Unit in January 1943 on the initiative of King George VI who wished all his subjects to witness with their own eyes the brave endurance that Malta was putting up in the face of impossible odds at a time when those courageous Maltese received the George Cross for bravery from him.

The film is narrated by Sir Laurence Olivier and features the purposely written 'Malta Suite' by the then King's Musician, Sir Arnold Bax. Using rare film footage taken by the filming units of all three services, Malta's war is chartered from Italy's entry into the war in 1940 until the lifting of the siege in 1942. Digital copies of this film are available from the museum.

The 'Malta at War Museum' is a fitting tribute to the hardships that Malta endured throughout the Second World War. It is open for visiting between 10.00 and 17.00 hrs daily. The tour comprises viewing of the unique 'Malta G.C.' original wartime documentary film and a guided tour into the deep and vast rock-cut tunnel maze that served as an underground civil defence centre for hundreds of families and an attractive display of period memorabilia collection.

Gozo

Gozo means 'Joy', and for me it has been aptly named because I always eagerly look forward to the joy I experience every time I visit Malta's little sister island. I have religiously done this every year since my relationship with the Maltese Islands began, and I have to say that its therapeutic sustenance has never waned. In fact, a few years ago, I became so besotted with this little island that I extended my vacation in Malta, and spent an extra two weeks in idyllic Xlendi Bay, from where I criss-crossed the rustic landscape every day; so pleasant and fulfilling that I could have stayed forever.

Gozo is only a short 15 minute ferry ride away from the mainland, but the crossing time seems even shorter thanks to the magnificent scenery on the approach. Stunning views of the island of Comino, Mgarr Harbour and the blue Mediterranean serves to whet my appetite for the old world charm and idyllic beauty that characterises this quaint and ancient island. But the views don't end with my arrival. Gozo's hilly landscape and panoramic countryside offers wonderful sightseeing opportunities. As I wander this green and mystic isle I'm treated to magnificent land and sea views stretching out for miles before my eyes.

First-time visitors to Gozo who are familiar with Malta's rather arid landscape are usually surprised, especially if they go during the spring or winter. The hilly landscape is far greener and more fertile than its big sister, and thanks to lower population density, the Island of Gozo is perfect for nature walks, bringing trekkers through some challenging and beautiful terrain.

Though separated from Malta by a mere 5km stretch of sea, Gozo is distinctly different. The island is a third the size of Malta, more rural and much more tranquil. Picturesque scenery, pristine coastline and untouched country trails adorn this little heaven. Magnificent baroque churches mushroom from the heart of small villages, and traditional farmhouses dot the rural landscape. Its culture and way of life are rooted in history and tradition and yet it is modern and self-sufficient.

Developed just enough but not too much, Gozo is a masterpiece wrought by nature and shaped by 7000 years of culture. Myth and reality meet here on what is believed to have been the Isle of Calypso in Homer's Odyssey, where the sea nymph held Odysseus (Ulysses) in her thrall for seven years.

Gozo has a long and colourful history. The Ġgantija Temples include some of the oldest sophisticated stone buildings on earth dating back over 5500 years. The fortified town of the Citadel that towers over Rabat (Victoria), combines Medieval layout with the buildings of the Knights of St John on a site inhabited since the Bronze Age.

Visitors will see farmers working their land, and meet 'cottage' entrepreneurs turning traditional activities into small businesses. Life on Gozo is tranquil and soft-paced and everyone has time for a chat. The pace picks up a little in the capital, Victoria, which has all the amenities of a modern town, and even here Gozo is casual and relaxed. But although the island brings great charm and tranquillity, this is no barrier to connectivity; there is excellent internet access across the island, with free WIFI in the main squares of all the villages.

Gozo is the epitome of a true Mediterranean holiday destination. Quaint villages with narrow streets, rustic bars and restaurants serving traditional food and wine, a peaceful village life, where time seems to tick slowly by, and where life's rhythms are dictated by the seasons, fishing and agriculture. But perhaps the most quintessentially Mediterranean characteristic of all found on this little island is hospitality and friendship. Gozitans are quieter, more understated and laid back than their Maltese cousins, but their warmth and welcome is the stuff of legend.

Gozo's attractions stretch well beyond the towns, villages and countryside.

It is one of Europe's top diving destinations with a remarkable range of shore as well as boat dives, all within easy reach of each other. Gozo has some world-class dive-sites. As well as awe-inspiring natural underwater landscapes, there are several sites where vessels have been scuttled creating interesting wrecks for divers to explore and new breeding grounds for marine life. Infrastructure servicing the diving industry has been amply developed on the island, which also boasts top medical services in this regard, including decompression facilities at the island's hospital. Testimonials from divers who keep coming back to the island, stress the holistic experience which only Gozo can offer.

There is so much for the visitor to discover in Gozo. From peaceful, well-restored farmhouses in picturesque villages to five-star luxury hotels, close encounters with nature on land and sea, to chats with friendly locals, breathtaking dive sites, to mouth-watering Mediterranean cuisine, and always the island's remarkable history and archaeology. There is something for everyone on the sun-drenched, warm-hearted eco-island of Gozo. If Odysseus arrived back today, I think he would be contented and happy to stay.

Gozo Highlights

Victoria

Victoria, or Rabat, which ever title it is given is a bustling little town in the centre of Gozo. While only 3km square with 7,000 inhabitants, the little capital is packed with quaint shops, traditional bars and exquisite restaurants. Victoria is not just the geographic heart of Gozo, it is also the centre of everyday activity. It manages to combine the bustle of its market and shops with a relaxed and sociable atmosphere. It is a great place to watch the Islanders go about their day, especially when the main market square, *It-Tokk*, comes to life.

This little square is a real gem; beautiful old buildings, quaint pubs and cafe bars, and a myriad of market stalls selling all kinds of everything. The atmosphere here is always buzzing and is usually enlivened even further by buskers and entertainers performing to the delight of tourists that come from all over the world.

Those visitors, having consumed the invigorating ambience of the square, then climb the energy-sapping hill to the medieval Citadel, with its fortifications, cathedral, museums and magnificent views. This is the centrepiece, not only of Victoria, but of the whole island. Towering majestically above the town since the fourteenth century, it can be seen from every corner of

Gozo, and when I walk around its massive bastions, I can see all of this idyllic island, its panorama of green landscape, and the blue Mediterranean encircling it.

Hidden away in a smaller square just behind It-Tokk in the heart of the old town is for me the greatest treasure of Gozo, St George's Basilica. This is the most richly adorned church in all of the Maltese Islands. Built between 1672 and 1678 it stands at the centre of a network of narrow, winding streets, its ornate baroque belfries, dome and transepts, all beautifully embellished, dominate the old square. The interior is just as magnificent, clad in marble with a canopied high alter similar to St Peter's Basilica in Rome. There are many gorgeous stained-glass windows in the dome and a treasure trove of wonderful works of art throughout. The dome and ceiling are the work of Roman artist Giovanni Battista Conti and other gems are by Mattia Preti, Guiseppe Cali and Stefano Erardi.

Most of the images are of various events in the life of St George to whom the church is dedicated. The real masterpiece and a must-see attraction is in the side chapel to the right of the high alter. It is a truly remarkable statue of St George, carved by Paolo Azzopardi in 1841 from a single tree trunk.

The location of this glorious church is also the old quarter of the town of Victoria. I love to spend lots of time strolling around this area. It takes me back in time when I wander over the little narrow walking streets winding their way through some of the most enchanting old architecture. I can admire ornate baroque townhouses dating from the 17th century, many with little niches holding statues of Our Lady and other favourite saints. To meander around these little winding alleys with their unique atmosphere and quaint old world charm would delight any visitor. This is the real heart of Gozo and I never tire of submitting to its alluring magnetism.

The Citadel

The Cittadella is an ancient fortified town located at the centre of Gozo, on a high hill overlooking the capital town of Victoria. Now a UNESCO World Heritage Site, its history dates from the late medieval era, but it was inhabited earlier in Neolithic times. The strategic location was ideal since the hill is naturally fortified, dominating the surrounding countryside while providing panoramic visuals over the whole island.

For centuries, the Citadel served as a sanctuary from attack by Barbary corsairs and Saracens. At several times during Gozo's history, these raiders took its population into slavery. After the Great Siege of 1565, the Knights set about re-fortifying the Citadel to provide refuge and defence against further attack. Until 1637, the Gozitan population was required by law to spend their nights within the Citadel for their own safety.

The fortifications which surround the Citadel served to protect the village communities from foraging corsairs who raided the Maltese islands in order to take slaves. The largest of these raids took place in July 1551, when a force of 10,000 Ottomans invaded Gozo and besieged the Citadel. The city capitulated after a few days of bombardment. Gozo's population of 5000 to 6000 people had taken refuge within the Citadel, and these were all taken as slaves when the city fell. With the exception of just 40 elderly and disabled citizens, the entire population of Gozo was chained and taken into slavery. It took nearly 50 years to re-populate the island and rebuild the Citadel in its present layout.

Today as I pass under the archway into the Citadel, I am welcomed by the majestic sight of Gozo Cathedral, standing tall in the small square at the top of a wide flight of steps guarded by two 17th-century bronze cannons. Very close by are several fascinating small museums: the Cathedral Museum, the Museum of Archaeology, the Folklore Museum, the Gozo Nature Museum, the Old Prison, the Old Gunpowder Magazine, the Grain Silos, the Battery and the World War II Shelter.

As I walk along the fortified ramparts I'm rewarded with a breathtaking 360-degree panoramic view of Gozo's hills and valleys, villages and churches and an exquisite view all the way across the sea to Malta. It takes a strenuous effort to climb the steep hill and the countless steps to reach the Citadel but having made the effort many times, I am always glad that I did, and eagerly look forward to returning.

Ta Pinu Basilica

Ta Pinu Basilica is located near the village of Gharb in the North Western Part of the island and is now Malta's national shrine, attracting pilgrims from all over the world. When I first discovered the sanctuary many years ago I was amazed at its effect on me. I experienced a strange peace and tranquillity, a solace and solitude that I had often yearned for, but only found it here in this little wayward and isolated beauty spot.

The origins of the Shrine of Our Lady of Ta Pinu are lost in the midst of time. The first records of its existence are in the archives of the Curia in Gozo, when Bishop Domenico Cubelles paid a visit to the chapel. This noted that the chapel had just been rebuilt and that it belonged to the noble family of 'The Gentile.'

When in 1575, the apostolic visitor Msgr. Pietro Duzina, delegated by Pope Gregory X11 to visit the Maltese Islands, paid his pastoral visit to the church, he found it was in a very bad state. He ordered the church to be closed and demolished and its incumbent duties to be passed to the parish church, today the cathedral of Gozo.

However, according to tradition when the workman struck the first blow with the pick he broke his arm. This was taken as an omen that the chapel had to be preserved and in fact this was the only chapel that survived Msgr. Duzina's decree ordering the demolition of similar chapels on the island.

In 1858 the church property changed hands and its name was changed to Ta Pinu. This was because Pinu Gauci became the procurator of the church and in 1611 he willingly offered money for its restoration. It was rebuilt with a stone altar and all liturgical services were provided. He also commissioned the painting of the Assumption of Our Lady for the main altar. This altarpiece was done in 1619 by Amadeo Perugino, probably a member of the inquisitor's train.

On the 22nd June 1883, Karmela Grima a forty-five year-old spinster and great devotee of the Blessed Virgin heard a call, while passing by the chapel on her return from the surrounding fields. "Come, come," she heard a woman's voice say. She was confused and frightened, and began to run away from the place. The voice called again, and this time Karmela realised that the voice was coming from within the chapel; she went inside and said her usual prayers. The voice which had come from the image of the Blessed Virgin asked her to recite three Ave Maria in honour of the three days her body remained in the tomb before her Assumption to Heaven.

Karmela did as the voice asked and went on her way. Shortly afterwards Karmela fell ill and remained confined to her bed for more than a year. After this time, Karmela revealed her secret to a friend, Francesco Portelli, who in turn told her that about the same time he also heard a woman's voice asking him to pray from within the chapel. Shortly after this mysterious call Francesco's mother was miraculously healed by the intercession of Our Lady of Ta` Pinu. The lonely chapel then became a place of pilgrimage for many people on the island and beyond.

Now, thousands of pilgrims from all over the world come and kneel before the ancient shrine of Our Lady of Ta Pinu, plead for cures and favours, and leave in peace, knowing that they have received a special blessing. Attached to the church is another shrine, this one dedicated to the thousands of anguished pilgrims from near and far who came with their afflictions, were cured, and returned with heartfelt gratitude to place on the shrine, pictures, mementoes, and their discarded aids; testament of the miracles performed for them by our Lady of Ta Pinu. St. Pope John Paul II visited the shrine in 1990, praying in the Chapel, celebrating mass and decorating an image of Our Lady with five golden stars. Pope Benedict XVI also prayed to Our Lady of Ta' Pinu on a visit to Malta in 2010.

Dwejra

Dwejra is a small location on the west coast just beyond the village of San Lawrenz. It is best known for its "inland sea" (small bay surrounded by high cliffs) and the Azure Window, a particular rock structure, and one of Malta's most loved attractions.

The name Dwejra comes from a small house which once stood on top of the cliffs surrounding the inland sea. With its unique features, the bay is a popular destination for tourists and local snorkelers and divers. The bay is home to a rich and diverse wildlife and underwater features, and has a very rugged feel.

The inland sea at Dwejra is a tiny bay surrounded by high cliffs and connected by a 60-metre long cave that leads out to the open sea. It's truly a place that evokes awe and always leaves a lasting impression. Several small boathouses can be found along the shoreline, housing the locals' fishing boats. You can take a boat trip through the cave, out to open sea and past the Azure Window and the nearby Fungus Rock.

The Azure Window is a unique rock shape in the form of an arch, which is found on the coastline near Dwejra. It's a popular location with scuba divers and a well-known feature and attraction in Gozo. In recent years parts of the structure have eroded and broken off and it is expected that the structure may collapse within a few years. In fact, although it's possible to walk on top of the Azure Window, several warning signs warn daredevils of the risks.

Fungus Rock, known locally as il-Gebla tal-General (The General's Rock), is a 60-metre high rock feature which is known for a particular type of flowery plant that was thought to possess medicinal value in the times of the Knights of St. John and was considered to be precious and of high value. Unauthorised access was punishable by death or life on the galleys and to make climbing the rock more difficult; Grandmaster de Pinto ordered the sides of the rock to be smoothed over. Despite its common name, it isn't actually a fungus, although its shape would easily have you believe it is. Because the plant is found mostly on Fungus Rock, the location is a nature reserve nowadays.

This is an area of Gozo of incredible beauty. Every visitor to the Maltese islands feels compelled to see those renowned attractions. The Azure Window has been featured in films, such as Clash of the Titans (1981) and The Count of Monte Cristo (2002). It can also be seen in the television miniseries: The Odyssey (1997), and HBO's TV series Game of Thrones.

The Ggantija Temples

Older than the Great Pyramid of Giza and Stonehenge, the twin temples of Ġgantija are amongst the oldest free-standing stone monuments in the world. Located near the village of Xaghra, they are a UNESCO World Heritage Site and attract thousands of visitors every year from every corner of the world.

The site consists of a megalithic complex of two temples surrounded by a massive common boundary wall and raised on a high terrace wall. The origins of Ggantija dates back to between 3600 and 3200 BC and being more than 5500 years old, they are the world's oldest free-standing structures, and the world's oldest religious structures, pre-dating the Pyramids of Egypt and Stonehenge.

Since some of the stones that comprise the dry-walls exceed five metres in length and weigh over 50 tons, it was believed in subsequent centuries that the edifice was the work of giants (Ġgant means 'giant' in Maltese), and that the bones of elephants and hippopotamuses found on the island were actually the remains of these mythical giants.

The temples were possibly the site of an Earth Mother Goddess Fertility Cult, with numerous figurines and statues found on site believed to be connected with that cult. Built with rough, coralline limestone blocks, each temple contains five apses connected by a central corridor leading to the innermost trefoil section.

Entrance to the Ġgantija Temples is from a newly constructed Interpretation Centre that provides visitors with the opportunity to explore various aspects related to life in the Neolithic. The centre is also home to a selection of the most significant finds discovered at various prehistoric sites in Gozo. The Interpretation Centre is linked to the temple site via an external pathway that provides visitors with unique views of the natural landscape that surrounds Ġgantija.

For visitors to the Maltese Islands, this is a not-to-be-missed attraction and here are the reasons why: (1) A UNESCO World Heritage Site. (2) One of Malta's best preserved prehistoric temples dating back to 3600/3200 BC. (3) Considered one of the oldest free standing monuments in the world. (4) They represent a phenomenal cultural, artistic and technological development in a very early period in human life. (5) An exhibition of some of the most unique prehistoric artefacts discovered in Gozo.

Ta Kola Windmill

Ta Kola Windmill is another tourist attraction in the village of Xaghra. It is one of the best preserved windmills in Gozo and dates back to the time of the Knights of St John in 1725. The Windmill's name Ta' Kola comes from the last miller, who was popularly known as Kola.

Throughout the centuries, the windmill was used by different families but in the 1980s it came into the ownership of the Grech family, who continued to run the windmill up until the 1980s. The construction of this windmill follows a plan which makes it similar to most windmills of that period found in Malta, consisting of a number of rooms on two floors surrounding the central cylindrical tower.

When the wind was blowing right for the mill to operate, the miller would send a signal to the villagers who would then bring their grain to be ground into flour. The heavy millstones can still be seen at the top of the mill linked to the central milling mechanism, around which the rooms where the miller lived and worked are located.

On the ground floor is the workshop with a vast array of historic tools, some of which were manufactured by the owners of the mill. On the first floor, the living quarters of the miller and his family have been recreated using traditional furniture and Gozitan crafts. You can visit the miller's dining room, bedrooms, and kitchen which are equipped with traditional utensils and cooking ware rarely seen today.

A visit to Ta Kola Windmill is an interesting little glimpse into the rural life of Gozo 300 years ago. It is now restored and open to the public. Visitors can get two historic attractions for the price of one in the village of Xaghra, as tickets are now available that will provide entrance to both the Ggantija Temples and the Ta Kola Windmill.

Ramla Bay

Renowned for its golden-red sand, Ramla Bay is situated in a fertile valley in the north of Gozo. It is a beautiful wide and sandy beach reached by a 45 minute walk from the village of Xaghra and by bus from Nadur and it is a popular tourist attraction. This is Gozo's, and arguably Malta's, best beach. A wide stretch of red sand, it is often referred to locally as "Ramla il-Ħamra" - the Red Sandy Beach! It is a wonderful place to swim, snorkel and chill out in the sun.

The area surrounding the beach of Ramla Bay provides scenic views of historical importance. Roman ruins are buried underneath the sand and Calypso Cave overlooks the western side of the beach. The Romans had built a villa here decorated with marble and stucco. It was so luxurious and refined that the building had its own hot bath supplied with water from a nearby spring.

Surrounded by hills on both sides, the sandy pathway on the eastern hillside leads to the Calypso Cave. According to the legend, this is the cave Homer refers to in 'The Odyssey' where the nymph, Ogygia lived, and where she entertained Ulysses for seven years before he moved ahead on his journey.

A notable landmark here is the statue of the Virgin Mary which was erected in the middle of the bay in 1881 and still stands there today. The area around the beach is undeveloped, although there are a couple of cafes and a stall set back from the beach. The sand dunes are protected and the valley leading down to the bay is green and fertile. The terraced walls built by the farmers give the valley an appearance of a quilt when viewed from surrounding high ground. Ramla Bay is a unique area that I have visited many times and is definitely one of the beauty spots of Gozo.

Gozo Villages

Mgarr Harbour

As the ferry approaches Mgarr Harbour I am always enthralled by the breathtaking charm of this gateway to the island of Gozo and its link to the outside world. I'm captivated by its picture-postcard natural setting. It is undoubtedly one of the most beautiful little harbours in all the Maltese Islands. Lines of colourful little fishing boats anchored in the dock, quaint honey-coloured houses, a tapestry of tiny green fields above, and the blue waters of the Mediterranean caressing the shore.

There is now a new pristine ferry terminal at Mgarr Harbour. It used to be a 'stone age' port facility dating back to 1841, but in recent years the government upgraded it at a cost of many millions of Euro and now it is state of the art. The mainland ferry port at Cirkewwa has also been fully modernised recently and both new terminals are now a great comfort to commuters and tourists. This big expenditure is fully justified by the huge numbers who use the service as the two ships carry 4 million passengers and over one million vehicles on 20,000 crossings each year.

Besides being Gozo's main harbour, Mġarr is one of the most important fishing villages of the island, providing the best shelter for the local fishing boats during the winter months. The village also has a modern yacht marina which hosts a large number of yachts and pleasure boats throughout the year. Overlooking the Harbour is Fort Chambrai, which was built by the Knights of St. John in 1749 and later used by the British forces. A church dedicated to Our Lady of Lourdes also overlooks Mġarr and typical of Mediterranean fishing ports, the harbour is very well served with restaurants and bars.

Xewkija

Having left Mgarr behind, the next stop on a visitor's tour of Gozo is Xewkija, the oldest village on the island with a population of 3,000 residents. It is highlighted on every tour because of its awesome rotunda, the circular church at the centre of the village which is Gozo's largest church with its massive dome a distinctive landmark, visible across much of the island.

The church, which claims to have the third largest unsupported dome in the world, was completed in 1971 after 20 years of building. It was dedicated to St. John the Baptist and replaced a seventeenth century church. Funded entirely by local donation and built mainly with labour from the village, the interior is stark and plain in comparison to the island's usual baroque decoration, but is spectacular for its enormous size.

In the impressive white limestone interior, eight concrete columns covered with stone support the elegant dome, which has an estimated weight of 45,000 tonnes. The interior shows off the versatility and texture of local limestone and the skills of local craftsmen. It is sparsely decorated with fine sculptures and modern paintings. The floor is of polished Carrara marble and the main altar is also carved in precious marble.

For me, one of the most intriguing aspects of this magnificent basilica is that the villagers built it around and over the existing church. When completed, they demolished the old church stone by stone and rebuilt it behind the new church. It is built exactly as it was for past centuries, but is now used as a church museum and is a wonderful little treasure to see and admire. Inside the old church there is a lift which visitors can use to take them up to the balcony of the dome for the most spectacular panoramic views of Gozo.

Gharb

Għarb is a village located at the westernmost point of the island of Gozo with a population of 1,500 people. It originated as a small hamlet centuries ago. The word Għarb is Arabic for west, so it should be no surprise that the village is the most westerly place on Gozo. One can see its ancient roots in the centre of the village where some houses have fine examples of decorated stone balconies.

Għarb is located in some of Gozo's most scenic countryside; it has become the image on many a postcard, its heavenly old square is charming and quintessentially Gozo, full of old world character. The square is dominated by a beautiful baroque parish church. Built between 1699 and 1729, it has an elegant façade and is dedicated to the Visit of Our Lady to her cousin St. Elizabeth, popularly known as the Feast of the Visitation. The feast day is on the 31st May each year and the Festa is held on the first weekend of July.

Għarb is a traditional village. Its character is distinctly rural and in the past its residents almost exclusively worked the surrounding fields in this fertile area of Gozo. They retained an old Maltese dialect, with a rich vocabulary of old words and pronunciations long since discarded by the rest of the population. Għarb is also renowned for its craftsmen, mostly famous for the manufacture of the unique 'Għarb blade', a tradiitonal sharp knife. Even today, Għarb is home to blacksmiths, locksmiths, cotton weavers and lace makers, carpenters and masters in cane-work. The village is also known for producing able fishermen, while Għarb shepherds produce the best Gozo Cheese on the Island.

It is a very appropriate place for the Gharb Folklore Museum, which occupies a historic house in the heart of the village. The 28 rooms contain all sorts of memorabilia linked with traditional trades, crafts and daily life. The building that houses the museum was once home to Frenc Mercieca (1892-1967), a saintly 'wise man' who cured many people with a mix of medicinal herbs and prayer to Our Lady. He left doctors perplexed by his successes and his reputation spread rapidly throughout the Maltese Islands and even abroad.

Also open to visitors is the former home of another saintly resident, Karmni Grima, the woman who heard the voice of Our Lady at Ta' Pinu and began the devotions that have turned it into Malta's most important shrine. Gharb and its green fertile hinterland is a quaint and beautiful place that I always look forward to visiting. I also like to wander up the hill opposite which has a steep but pleasant path leading to the top, adorned with white marble statues of the Stations of the Cross. Also close to Gharb is the Ta' Dbiegi Crafts Village, where various handicrafts are made and sold. Visitors can watch craftspeople creating mouth-blown glass, Gozo lace, pottery and filigree, and of course like me, take some home with you as a memento of your joyous visit to Gozo.

San Lawrenz

San Lawrenz is another charming and traditional village located in the westerly part of the island, not far from Dwejra Bay and Ta' Dbiegi Craft Village. This picturesque village, with a population of only 750 residents, is surrounded by three hills: Ghammar, Gelmus, and Dbiegi, which at 195 metres above sea level is Gozo's highest point.

The village is characterised by lots of beautiful 17th century houses, many with elaborately carved stone balconies and the residents have succeeded in retaining its traditional and rural lifestyle. It has managed to embrace modern progress without sacrificing its natural beauty and those values and traditions which form the identity of this charming village. You will find here the stark contrast of a typically rural lifestyle and nurtured village traditions against the five star luxury of the Kempinski San Lawrenz Hotel on the outskirts of the village.

Like every village in Gozo, San Lawrenz has its own impressive parish church. Built in 1893 in baroque style, the San Lawrenz Church contains many beautiful works of art by well-known local artists such as the renowned Guiseppe Cali. The feast of San Lawrenz falls in the first week of August and like all other villages, the residents celebrate their traditional Village Festa around that time.

On my way back from enjoying the delights of Dwejra, I always stop and linger awhile in this quaint little village of San Lawrenz. It is a heavenly spot and I wasn't surprised to discover that this is where the world famous British writer and novelist, Nicholas Monsarrat, spent his final years. I suppose that for an icon of the waves, who gave the world 'The Cruel Sea,' it was no surprise that he chose this peaceful little hamlet, overlooking the blue Mediterranean, to end his days. Like myself, he loved the Maltese Islands, and his other great masterpiece, 'The Kappillan of Malta,' recalling the 'World War Two' heroism of the Maltese people, was written in this little hideout.

Though sadly, the master is now gone, his simple dwelling is still here, and when I pause and ponder, I'm always filled with awe, remembering the literary genius that once graced this spot, and seeing the view he enjoyed from his writing desk by the window. I'm not surprised by his decision to be buried at sea – for a legendary sea-lover, what could be more appropriate. Appropriate and fitting too, was the decision of the villagers to name one of their little streets 'Triq Nicholas Monsarrat,' a tribute to a world famous legend, and an appreciation of his affection for Malta, Gozo, and especially San Lawrenz.

Xaghra

Xaghra is a picturesque village, rich in historical heritage and surrounded by fertile valleys with some of the best agricultural land in Gozo. Set on a plateau 140 metres above sea level, it is the third largest village in Gozo, having a population of around 4,000 people.

As I have described in a previous chapter, Xaghra is home to some wonderful historical attractions. The world famous Ggantija Temples, the amazing Ramla Bay beach with its red sand, the mythical Calypso's Cave, the fascinating Ta' Kola Windmill and two other interesting caves, Xerri's Grotto and Ninu's Cave are all located around this ancient village. Another Xaghra attraction that should not be missed is the Pomskizillious Museum of Toys, with a display of antique toys and a waxwork of artist and rhyme-writer Edward Lear.

A Medieval chapel dedicated to St Anthony Abbot was Xaghra's first parish church after it gained parish status in 1688 and still stands. The much larger Basilica that dominates the central square and serves the parish today is dedicated to the Nativity of the Blessed Virgin Mary. It is one of the most beautiful of Gozo's churches, with its richly decorated interior, gilt sculptures, Italian marbles and paintings. The Village Festa is celebrated every 8th September, which besides being the feast of the Nativity of Our Lady is also "Il-Festa tal-Vittorja", The Victory Feast, commemorating the victory of the Maltese under the Knights of St. John over the Ottoman Turks in the Great Siege of 1565.

Xaghra has lots of shops, restaurants and cafe bars. The village square, dominated by the magnificent parish church, is brimming with character and fascination with its quaint narrow streets designed like fingers radiating from its centre. It is a pleasant little place for a leisurely stroll or to enjoy a nice quiet little drink in a relaxing ambience surrounded by natural unspoilt beauty.

Nadur

Nadur sits on the hills above a fertile valley, once the hunting grounds of Grand Master Wignacourt but now the fruit growing district of the island. It has a population of about 5000 people, which makes it the second most populated village in Gozo. It is an interesting traditional village and affords fabulous views over land and sea. It is reached either from Victoria or directly from Mġarr Harbour. Renowned for the enchanting green valleys and peaceful bays that surround it; on the coast nearby are the beautiful beaches of San Blas and Ramla as well as Daħlet Qorrot, a delightful small bay very popular with fishermen as well as local swimmers.

There are about 20 farmers in Nadur, the majority of who work their fields on a part-time basis. From the orchards of Nadur come most of the local fruits such as plums, peaches, apples, oranges and lemons. It was recently put on record that 70% of all Maltese citrus originates from Nadur and the local council is presently promoting the planting of olive trees imported from Italy as these trees have consistently decreased in numbers over a period of years. Some residents of the village earn their living from the sea as fishermen or sailors but many others work in business or professional services in Gozo or on the mainland.

The parish church is dedicated to St. Peter and St. Paul. It is an exceptional monument, both in terms of architecture and paintings, marble works and decorations. The church was designed by the Maltese architect Giuseppe Bonnici and constructed at the highest point in Nadur in 1760. The precious titular statue of St. Peter and St. Paul was made in Marseille in 1882. It is a masterpiece that adorns the church, and it is taken out for a procession during the Village Festa, which is celebrated annually on the 29th of June.

The village of Nadur is renowned for its Annual Carnival, which unlike the more festive occasions in other locations takes on a sombre and dark mood because of the macabre costumes. Nadur Carnival is a unique event characterised by the spontaneity and creativity of all those taking part.

Situated in such a strategic location, Nadur has played a vital part in the defence of Gozo for many centuries. During the time of the Knights, a watch tower was built called Dahlet Qorrot Tower. Another tower named

Kenuna Tower was built by the British in the 19th century, linking Malta and Gozo with a telegraph link. From the top of this tower, there are incredible views of Gozo, Comino and the Northern part of Malta. The new Maltese Garden at Kenuna makes this area a must-see for all visitors. Another attraction worth visiting in Nadur is the Kelinu Grima Maritime Museum which houses an interesting collection of naval artifacts from the old Nadur trade of seafaring.

Marsalforn

Marsalforn is one of the most popular resorts on the Island of Gozo. In summer it pulses with life as hundreds of Gozitan and Maltese families move in to spend time at the coast and foreign visitors arrive for the refreshing therapy of sun and sea.

A cute little beach of sand and small pebbles, it is flanked by a promenade which runs around the head of the bay, providing a pleasant gathering place for local families and visitors alike. The rocks along each side of the bay provide plenty of additional space for sunbathing, swimming or snorkelling. Marsalforn is also a popular base for diving enthusiasts, who can choose from a variety of diving schools and dive sites. The village is also well served with some beautiful restaurants, cafe bars, self-catering apartments and hotels.

Marsalforn is located on the north coast of Gozo, The village lies between the hill-top towns of Xagħra and Żebbuġ and forms part of the locality of Żebbuġ. To the south of Marsalforn is a fertile valley named after the village. The valley is bounded by several hillocks and used to be known as the "haven of hillocks". The most famous of these is tas-Salvatur (Our Saviours Hill) due to the legends surrounding it, recorded by Giovanni Abela in the 17th Century.

This volcano like hill has captured the attention of the people since 1901, when a large wooden cross was erected on its peak. Three years later, when Gozo was consecrated to Christ the Saviour, a stone statue of Christ replaced the cross. This was in turn replaced by a gigantic concrete statue towering twelve metres above the hill, which remains to this day.

As recorded in the Acts of the Apostles, Paul the Apostle was shipwrecked in Malta, but legend maintains that it was from Marsalforn that he embarked for Sicily and Rome. Today, this legend is symbolised by the village's emblem, which consists of a viper encircling a sword. This refers to an episode involving Saint Paul when he remained unharmed after being bitten by a viper. The village church of 'Saint Paul Shipwreck' is also dedicated to the memory of Saint Paul's departure from Marsalforn. The church, originally raised in the fourteenth century, has been rebuilt and enlarged many times. The foundation stone of the present church was laid in 1730. The feast is celebrated on 10 February.

Marsalforn is one of the most popular beaches in Gozo, providing an ideal place to swim, sunbathe and enjoy the Mediterranean climate. In summer it is buzzing with life, fun and exhilaration. Many families from Malta and Gozo have summer houses here and often spend the whole season by the sea. The traditional Maltese Luzzu fishing boats give Marsalforn Bay a charming and cosy feel and they also provide the restaurants in the bay with fresh succulent seafood. I visit Marsalforn during the quiet seasons and I always find it a friendly and relaxing little place, hidden away from the big outside world, where I can linger and rest in perfect peace and tranquillity.

Zebbug

This picturesque village, not to be confused with the village in Malta of the same name, home to around 3,000 people, is perched on a tranquil hill in the north of Gozo with panoramic views of the countryside and the Mediterranean. Zebbug is Maltese for Olive Tree and therefore one would assume that the name derives from the wild olives that grew plentifully in the area. The village has expanded and has become a popular holiday destination for both Maltese and overseas' visitors because it offers spectacular panoramic views. A steep and scenic road leads downhill to the coastline below at Qbajjar Bay and on to the fishing port and tourist resort of Marsalforn.

On a slope at the edge of the village, facing Ġurdan Lighthouse and known as 'The Wild Thyme Field' a considerable deposit of onyx marble was found in 1738. Many churches in Malta and Gozo have works of art made from this onyx, but Żebbuġ church is by far the most spectacular. It is covered with this semi-precious stone. The high altar, the choir, and the baptistery are all sculpted out of this marble. The parish church, dedicated to Santa Marija (St Mary) the Assumption, was consecrated in 1726 and apart from the cathedral in Victoria, it is the oldest parish church to be consecrated in Gozo.

The long history of the community here is evident in the strong traditional culture prevalent in the village. This is apparent in the deep devotion the villagers have for their Church, in the careful maintenance of the many little street niches (shrines) which contain holy figures to watch over the narrow winding streets, and also in the production of high quality traditional crafts such as lace, basket weaving and woollen blankets. Until quite recently, agriculture, wool and loom were the main occupations in Zebbug.

This is a pleasant little village with lots of character and charm. It is beautifully located in a picturesque area of Gozo and is further enhanced by the proximity of some picturesque coastal gems.

Xlendi Bay

The idyllic landlocked bay of Xlendi and its glorious blue green waters were for many years a haunt of artists and photographers. Xlendi Bay, (pronounced 'Shlen-di') is a little haven of quaint charm. Beautifully placed at the end of a deep lush ravine which was once a river bed and hidden by two tall rocky promontories, it is a delight for swimming, diving, or just strolling around. During summer, the sheltered little dock is packed with a myriad of pleasure craft, but in winter, only the little boats of the local fishermen are here. In peak season too, the dozens of little bars, cafes, and restaurants are crowded, but many of them close for the winter months. I like to come to this beauty spot during the quiet season. The towering high rocks, the blue of the ocean, the little boat repair yard, and the scenic beauty of it all, can be viewed and appreciated much better in the absence of an overcrowded mass of tourists.

That's why I came here for two weeks a few years ago and enjoyed the comfort and quietness of 'St. Patrick's Hotel.' I savoured every minute of my fourteen days, strolling the hills and valleys, rambling through the old lanes and little fields, absorbing the soothing peace and solitude of this world apart. From this homely base, I navigated my little car to every corner of the island, and when it was time for me to say goodbye, I felt blissfully revived, happy, refreshed and inspired.

The Bay of Xlendi always retains its peaceful atmosphere and is surprisingly undeveloped though there is a good choice of accommodation with lots of apartments and hotels. Xlendi is flanked by steep cliffs. For some of the most spectacular views, I climb the stairs up the cliffs to the right or cross the little bridge over the ravine on my left where I can meander around this gorgeous plateau beside the ancient Xlendi Tower. Bathing in Xlendi is usually off the rocks along the bay with access down ladders into the deep crystal clear water. On the left side of the bay, two tiers of pathways provide for both a walkway and a flat space to relax and sunbathe.

Fontana

On the main road halfway between Victoria and Xlendi sits the cosy little village of Fontana. Overlooking the green and fertile Lunzjata Valley, with about 1,000 residents, the village is famous for its fresh water springs. It was once part of the capital, Victoria, but is now a suburb and a parish in its own right. Fontana (Italian for spring) was first inhabited because of the availability of fresh water and in the sixteenth century, arched shelters were built over each spring for the convenience of the people using them. These are still standing today and inside there are traditional stone water tubs in which local folk did their daily washing. Those washhouses are still operating today, and the locals can sometimes be seen doing their laundry there.

On the lower part of Fontana, on the right-hand side of the road to Xlendi Bay, I like to stop and admire the tapestry of little fields growing luscious vegetables and watch the local farmers doing their labour of love planting and nurturing them. They use a very old irrigation system made up of stone gutters and this constantly brings water from the springs to feed and irrigate the crops.

The earliest settlers of Fontana were mainly farmers and hunters, but there were also a few fishermen that fished out of the nearby Xlendi Bay. It was the fishermen who set aside some of their profits to built the parish church in the late 19th century. The church, dedicated to the Sacred Heart, was established as a parish in 1911. The village celebrates the Festa annually around the 2nd week of June.

Fontana village is must-stop location for all tour coaches and tourists. The unique springs and the washhouses are a big attraction but another delight of the village is the presence of a wonderful arts and crafts shop and an upmarket jewellery shop. The craft shop is crammed with the most beautiful handcrafts especially the world famous handmade Maltese lace. Whenever I'm in the area I always make a visit to this delightful place and I never tire of watching in awe at those gifted Maltese women weaving their intricate way to creating an item of beautiful lace.

Kercem & Santa Lucija

The villages of Kerċem and Santa Lucija are close together at the south-east edge of the capital Victoria and are surrounded by the most beautiful inland landscapes in Gozo. Spread between the picturesque Lunzjata Valley, the green hills of Mixta, Għar Ilma and Dbieġi, and stretching up to the Pond of San Rafflu and the Xlendi cliffs, this is an ideal place for artists, walkers and cyclists.

The village of Kercem has a population of around 1700 people and archaeological discoveries have shown that the area was one of the earliest places to be inhabited in Gozo, beginning some 7,000 years ago. The parish church, built in 1851 and enlarged in 1906-10, is dedicated to both St Gregory and to Our Lady of Perpetual Help. As a result the village has two Festas each year, in March for St Gregory and on the second Sunday in July for Our Lady of Perpetual Help.

The peaceful hamlet of Santa Lucija, although adjoining Kercem, is quite distinct with its quaint rustic church square and peaceful atmosphere displaying a calm picturesque charm unsurpassed throughout the whole island. Here we find the warmest hearted locals with a welcoming air and a passion for their heritage. The little hamlet nestles between three hills, each having a natural water spring, making its surroundings one of the most fertile areas of Gozo. The feeling of tranquillity in the area is almost tangible, and the enchanting surroundings make it perfect for those who choose to explore its beautiful countryside. The local community has also proudly preserved old crafts and cultural heritage such as pottery, remains of a medieval settlement, a 19th century aqueduct and a fountain supplying natural water.

Santa Lucija Parish Church, dedicated to Saint Lucy, was first recorded in 1575, and rebuilt from its foundations in the 1790's; the latest enlargement taking place in 1950. Saint Lucy is invoked by those who have problems with their eyesight, and many flock to the church on the 13th of December, this being the feast day of the patron saint. The village square is dominated by the church and by an impressive traditional stone cross.

A number of old farmhouses in the area have been discreetly converted to country villas, with great care taken to retain a rustic look. Santa Lucija is one of the many unspoilt places in Gozo whose residents stubbornly retain their laid back traditional way of life and for a visitor like me who cherishes the old way; their efforts fill me with pleasure and enchantment.

Munxar

Munxar (pronounced Moon-shar) is a tiny village of just about 700 people which lies south-west of the capital Victoria. Munxar is the Maltese word for Bucksaw - a saw set in an adjustable H-shaped frame used for sawing firewood on a buck, and the village gets its name from the imagery suggested by the landscape where it is set, wedged between two valleys: Ghancija valley on the Munxar side and Xlendi valley on the Fontana side. The ravine was in fact a river bed in the ice age and although the village itself has numerous links with the sea, it lies safely inland in one of the most scenic areas of Gozo.

Like all Gozo villages the square in Munxar is dominated by the elegant parish church. This beautiful basilica, built in 1925 and dedicated to St Paul's Shipwreck was consecrated in the village when it was declared an official parish in 1957. A parish centre was also built in 1972 and this became the hub of most of the social, religious, cultural and recreational activities of the village.

The devout faith and religious fervour of the villagers of Munxar is reflected in the holding of five annual processions each year by this small but closely knit community. The first is on the Sunday nearest the 10th of February known as the Quarant'Ore. On the Friday preceding Palm Sunday, Our Lady of Sorrows is invoked, on the last Sunday of May the statue of St Paul is carried through the village with pomp and glory, and then in mid-

June it is the feast of Corpus Cristi. Finally, on the first Sunday of October, it is the turn of Our Lady of the Rosary to be celebrated and honoured. These events ensure that the villagers and the saints are kept in close contact, and that visitors who arrive at those times can enjoy an intriguing insight into the village culture.

Throughout the years, Munxar has established its own unique features and retained its charm and character. When wandering through this beautiful area I always linger a while there to savour the typical village ambience and taste the unique rural spirit of another hidden treasure of the Island of Gozo.

Comino

Comino is a rocky wilderness, with jagged cliffs, two small sandy beaches, coves, creeks and a coastline dotted with deep caves. And of course, Comino Island is known for the famous Blue Lagoon bay with its crystal clear and azure-coloured water. With a permanent population of just four residents, one visiting priest and a policeman, this rugged little hideaway conjures up pleasant thoughts of dreamy island happiness. Indeed, only a few minutes from Malta's mainland, the island of Comino presents an interesting little odyssey and a day trip of pleasant surprises.

Named after the plentiful cumin (flowering plant) that grows on the island, Comino is thick with wild herbs and flowers, with the entire island classified as a wildlife sanctuary nowadays. It is mostly visited by tourists for a day trip while some of the more adventurous Maltese people visit Comino to camp or hike across the island.

The island was inhabited in the Roman period, but did not have much significance until the Knights of St John arrived. It then had a dual role: hunting grounds for the Knights and a staging post in the defence of the Maltese Islands against the Ottoman Turks. It had proved a useful base for pirates operating in the central Mediterranean and, though stark and barren today, it was home to wild boar and hares when the Knights arrived in 1530.

The Grandmasters went to great lengths to ensure that their game on Comino was protected: anyone found breaking the embargo on hunting could expect to serve three years rowing on a galley. After World War II, Comino remained a backwater until its fortunes revived with tourism in the mid-1960s.

Although most famous for the Blue Lagoon, with its sheltered bay of shimmering, clear water and easily accessible through the several boat trip operators in Malta or Gozo, there is much more to see beyond the lagoon. Comino is steeped in caves, creeks and grottos which lend themselves well to scuba diving, snorkelling and swimming, with many sunken treasures around as these caves were popular with corsairs (pirates) in the Middle Ages.

Comino has no cars or tarmac roads, has one hotel, a tiny ancient chapel and a small police station. But in summer it is a major tourist attraction offering a complete change of pace from the neighbouring islands of Malta and Gozo and is a great place to go for a day trip, or even to spend part of a holiday, especially for those who cherish peace and tranquillity.

Conclusion

I hope you have enjoyed this treasure-hunting trip to the Maltese Islands sitting in the heart of the Mediterranean. I have certainly enjoyed sharing with you some of the delights of these charming little islands. With a church for every day of the year and a feast for every weekend of the summer, a warm sunny climate, golden beaches, a rich culture and a glorious historical background which dates back 7,000 years, you couldn't but be impressed, intrigued and enchanted.

In this little book I have endeavoured to unveil the hidden treasures of the Maltese Islands. Many guide books are crammed with useful information for tourists visiting the islands and I use them myself. But I have always felt that these guide books don't get to the heart of Malta and the Maltese people. Having been a regular visitor for many years I have now discovered all those little hidden gems that make the islands so captivating and wonderful. I have also seen tourists here for a short stay and wondering how to get the most from their visit. I hope this little book will guide them to the heart and soul of the Maltese Islands and like me, be inspired and enchanted as a result.

So now, I have taken you on our little trek through this idyllic paradise of history, beauty and intrigue. Before we began I posed the question: what is it about the Maltese Islands that brings an Irishman back year after year, fills him with joy and enchantment, and sends him home restored, revitalised, and eagerly looking forward to his next visit?

In our little journey through the hidden treasures of those enchanting islands, I hope I have given you some clues to help you answer that question. It's really only a tiny taste and a bird's-eye view of my little haven of tranquillity. But we have seen the mystique and beauty of its landscape, the intrigue and fascination of its history and the simplicity and sincerity of its people. The pen does not adequately convey these characteristics; they must be seen and experienced in reality.

I have always felt that there is something unique and exceptional about the Maltese people. Perhaps their strength is derived from centuries of defensive heroism against greedy predators, and their eventual glorious triumphs over pain and adversity. Whatever drives them,

Malta is now a strong Independent Republic, with a healthy democracy, a prosperous economy, a proud distinctive culture, and a deep-rooted Christianity that inspires all their thoughts, hopes and deeds.

By now you have probably figured out why I titled this little book 'In Love with Malta.' As you may have gathered, I have been in love with Malta for many years and have always felt blessed to have discovered this little paradise. It is my 'home from home' and I'm so pleased to have found it that I now gladly share it with the millions of other lucky tourists who have discovered it too.

To conclude, I would like to repeat the little thought contained in the last paragraph of my first travel book on Malta. "Some famous geologists have speculated that the Maltese Islands, being just a little 'rockscape' peeping above the waves of the Mediterranean, may be susceptible to an earthquake, or a future giant Tsunami, and could be submerged into oblivion in minutes. I can never see that happening. If courage, piety, honesty, and sincere generosity, are virtues recorded on high as bonus points, Malta will prevail into the distant future, in peace and prosperity, illuminating the Mediterranean as a beacon of light for the world."

The End

It's a Long Way to Malta

An Irishman's 'Gem in the Med'

Paddy Cummins

The 2013 Number One Malta Travel Book.

"Paddy Cummins has created a gripping and emotional book that captivates at every turn of the page.

Endlessly fascinating, tensely absorbing, with humorous anecdotes.

This is classic travel writing – a brilliant read"

Michael K Hayes. Renowned Travel Writer. BBC Radio Presenter.

www.amazon.com/dp/B008QNJJBE

The Crying Sea

Paddy Cummins

A Maltese fishing boat explodes in a raging inferno and sinks to the depths of the Mediterranean.

So begins six days and nights of unspeakable anguish for the crew; shock, horror and grief for the island of Malta.

Inspired by a true 2008 sea disaster. A harrowing story of intense human drama.

"A superb read ... A story that will remain with you forever."

Damien Tiernan. Author of:

'Souls Of The Sea'

www.amazon.com/dp/B009A8G64C

This true story is now a major film

'SIMSHAR'

Other books by
Paddy Cummins

At Home in Ireland

Fields of Green

The Bombing of Campile

Yoke the Pony

The Crying Sea

It's a Long Way to Malta

Time & Tide

Green Lodge

Dream Valley

The Long Road

Doctor Google

27273720R00136

Printed in Great Britain
by Amazon